KU-628-962

RUNES
Made Easy

Also in the *Made Easy* series

RUNES
Made Easy

Harness the Magic of the
Ancient Northern Oracle

RICHARD LISTER

HAY HOUSE

Carlsbad, California • New York City
London • Sydney • New Delhi

Published in the United Kingdom by:
Hay House UK Ltd, The Sixth Floor, Watson House,
54 Baker Street, London W1U 7BU
Tel: +44 (0)20 3927 7290; Fax: +44 (0)20
3927 7291; www.hayhouse.co.uk

Published in the United States of America by:
Hay House Inc., PO Box 5100, Carlsbad, CA 92018-5100
Tel: (1) 760 431 7695 or (800) 654 5126
Fax: (1) 760 431 6948 or (800) 650 5115; www.hayhouse.com

Published in Australia by:
Hay House Australia Pty Ltd, 18/36 Ralph St, Alexandria NSW 2015
Tel: (61) 2 9669 4299; Fax: (61) 2 9669 4144; www.hayhouse.com.au

Published in India by:
Hay House Publishers India, Muskaan Complex,
Plot No.3, B-2, Vasant Kunj, New Delhi 110 070
Tel: (91) 11 4176 1620; Fax: (91) 11 4176 1630; www.hayhouse.co.in

Text © Richard Lister, 2021

The moral rights of the author have been asserted.

All rights reserved. No part of this book may be reproduced by
any mechanical, photographic or electronic process, or in the form
of a phonographic recording; nor may it be stored in a retrieval
system, transmitted or otherwise be copied for public or private
use, other than for 'fair use' as brief quotations embodied in articles
and reviews, without prior written permission of the publisher.

The information given in this book should not be treated as
a substitute for professional medical advice; always consult a
medical practitioner. Any use of information in this book is at the
reader's discretion and risk. Neither the author nor the publisher
can be held responsible for any loss, claim or damage arising out
of the use, or misuse, of the suggestions made, the failure to take
medical advice or for any material on third-party websites.

A catalogue record for this book is available from the British Library.

Tradepaper ISBN: 978-1-78817-642-2
E-book ISBN: 978-1-78817-646-0
Audiobook ISBN: 978-1-78817-643-9

Interior illustrations: pages 1, 21, 187 Jaanus Jagomägi/Unsplash;
all other images © Richard Lister.

Printed and bound in Great Britain by
TJ Books Limited, Padstow, Cornwall

This book is dedicated to the God of Kings, The Wanderer, The Furious One, Mr Wednesday, Odin.

To Leanne and Sarah for their encouragement and passion.

And to my radiant wife, Lisa, without whose constant support and guidance, these words would not see reality.

As you sit in your safe home,
surrounded by peace, comfort,
and the trappings of civilization,
do you, reader, remember the energies of old,
the memories once filled with passion and power?
Even now, after hundreds of years,
do they remain glowing, radiant with the glitter of
the midnight sun
Or do they then darken, like bloodstains on the
annals of history?

Can your mind, slow with sleep and delirium,
direct your soul back to the joys and pain of the
past...

...Then follow me,
I will lead you down that path.
Though...
Your heart will guide you better than I.
Upon that I rely, and so we begin.

Z. TOPELIUS, *THE SURGEON'S STORIES*, 1836
TRANSLATED BY RICHARD LISTER

Contents

PART III: HOW TO WORK WITH THE RUNES

Preface

From the outset, I want to make it clear that this book is guidance based on my own study, practice and experience. Take what I say and work with it, grow with it in a way that feels good to you. Fill the void with your own experience and power.

What I want for you to get from this book is a relationship with the runes that will let you use them – the runes that have been used for thousands of years to communicate, divine and heal. Use them as a modality to access your power, creativity and joy. Use them to realize that it's simply social conditioning that leads us to behave in certain ways, and that you are completely allowed, in fact, actively encouraged, to bend and form the rules and empower yourself to be the awesome and sovereign human being you were born to be.

First, I'd like you to know me, where my bias is, what has led me here and why you would benefit from putting your trust and energy into what I have to say in this book.

I'm a man, born and raised in Kent in England. I'm 6 feet 7 inches and big. I have a beard and have spent a lot of the last 15 years dressed as a Viking. 'Vikingness' literally runs in my blood and bones. My ancestry goes back to the Normans and then further back still to the Norwegian Vikings of Göngu-Hrólfr.

I discovered 'Heathen paganism' at university, and it felt good – a remembrance, as it were. This led me to the runes.

One night I was at a pagan camp in a field in the middle of an ancient forest. Most people had gone to sleep and the diehards were the only ones left around the fireside.

This next bit is going to sound weird, but it's true. So, shush.

I had a vision, a full-blown deity-standing-in-the-fire vision, telling me to go and learn ancestral medicine and healing techniques, so I could serve better. The deity had one eye and a spear: Odin, Nordic king of the gods, god of war and shamanic healing.

I was shaken to the core. I stood staring into the fire for what felt like hours before taking myself off to my tent.

This was to be the first of many visits from Odin, and since that first vision, two crows, Huginn and Muninn, have often made themselves known to me as well, to make sure I'm heeding the call.

Let's be clear: when Odin speaks, I listen.

So, over the last decade and a half, I have dedicated myself to healing. In all its forms: I've worked in a hospital Accident and Emergency Department, trained as a nurse, trained as a yoga teacher, learned the ancient practices of Ayurveda and massage, and studied NLP, psychology and trauma, and throughout that time, I've worked with the runes and their guidance, wisdom, medicine and magic daily, in both my personal practice and my work with clients.

Why?

Because they hold medicine for these times.

The runes aren't fortune-tellers, they're way-showers, and in a world where we are feeling stripped of our power, they give it back to us; the power to look into the mists of the future, to support and heal ourselves, and/or have the self-insight to seek the right direction/people/help.

So, you could say that Odin made me do it. Odin made me write this rune book to support you so that you too will remember, in the same way that I did, the magic and medicine and personal power held in the runes.

Thanks, Odin.

Introduction

In a time before Christianity came to the north, a time when people clung to a precarious existence on the harsh, sparse soil of the frozen fjords, power was etched into stone.

This power was gifted from the gods and goddesses to the people to help them communicate, cast spells, divine the future and memorialize their lives.

This power came in the form of runes.

Runes are a series of lines carved in rock, bone, metal or wood to convey meaning and energy. These ancient sigils – mystic lines and symbols – are found all over Scandinavia, and their use was so prolific that they extended their reach down through France to the Mediterranean, all over Britain, and even, according to some, to Canada.

They started off relatively basic, with concepts drawn from their users' surroundings: beasts that stalked the lonely woodlands, thorns that ripped flesh, wood that grew. Community, family, seasons and elements are all held within the shapes and symbols of the earliest runes, the Elder Futhark, that were used 1,700 years ago.

Futhark

Just as we call our series of letters 'the alphabet', so the series of runes is called 'the Futhark'.

Our alphabet has this name because the first letter in Greek is Alpha, 'A', and the second is Beta, 'B'. Alphabet.

Futhark is exactly the same – a word built out of the sounds of the first runic symbols.

F, U, Th, A, R and K: Futhark.

As time rolled on, people changed, and the runes changed too. Different parts of Europe had slightly different versions, which grew from the different peoples' interactions with nature, the gods and cosmic energy. Different languages brought the need to make the rune names fit the sounds that people were hearing and speaking. In Scandinavia, the Elder Futhark became the Younger Futhark, a smaller set of runes with more abstract ideas. In Britain, the Saxons, Angles, Jutes and Northumbrians had their own songs of the runes, and Northumbria even had extra runes. Denmark and the people around the Balkans also had their own take on the message of the runes. But the runes were still used for communication, for divination, to provide guidance and support, and were also bound together to make runic spells.

Then, as Christianity spread, the ways of worship changed, the ways of making letters changed, and the mighty rune stones began to grow moss. Their energy lay dormant for hundreds of years.

Empires rose and fell, wars raged across the lands, society changed. Still the energy of the runes lay dormant, apart from in a few isolated areas.

Now, people are beginning to work with the runes once again and their power is reawakening. Their energy is beginning to flow through the land, the people. The aurochs and the hero are finding their place in a new world.

In this book, I cover the ancient names, sounds and energetic patterns of the Elder Futhark. I've chosen this pattern of runic energy because its sounds resonate with modern Anglophone people and there are lots of examples of rune stones from all over Norway, Sweden and northern Britain that we can go and see and even touch.

Remember now, as you read on, that the runic energies you will encounter are old and they are desperate to become part of the world again. They have a hunger to be used, to be active and to pulse, as they once did, with the vital energy of life. They desire, no, they *require* us to bring our current view and perspective to their energy, and to use that energy in a way that is helpful and supportive in these times. The giant ox of ancient Scandinavia may no longer walk this planet, but there are other creatures and constructs with which the rune Uruz resonates.

This is the challenge for us: what do the runes mean in today's world?

By picking up this book and opening its pages, you have chosen to take up that challenge. So, your responsibility, once you've finished reading, is to take your magic, use the runic constructs and vibrations and work with them to develop ways in which they can support us all in the here and now.

The tree of the runes is rooted, strong and stable, ready to grow and support the needs of the world. It's time for us to connect and work with the ancient wisdom of the runes and use their power, medicine and guidance to navigate these times.

Why runes are my favourite thing, and why they could be yours too

From moss-covered stone carvings in Denmark and Norway to etched steel in London and Paris, even the hallowed building of the Hagia Sophia in Turkey, runes have fascinated people throughout history. What makes them so special for me is that they evoke the primal energy and magic of the ancient people of the north and the land they inhabited, from the ancient aurochs moodily stalking the moors to the great god Thor flashing lightning across the night sky to slay the ice giants, to the laughter of children around the hearth fire on a cold winter's night.

The runes are some of the most powerful divination, communication and support tools available to us, and when we learn how to work with them and their connection to the energy of the *Wyrd*, the universe, they can provide much-needed support and guidance in our daily lives.

What will you get from this book?

To understand where we are going with the runes, we must first understand where we've been. So this book is designed to share the basic concepts and designs of the ancient Nordic magical and spiritual path, as well as the runes themselves, their many possible meanings and some of the mythology associated with them.

The ancient Nordic mind was different from our modern one, so we need to step back into the Nordic world as it was when the runes were originally gifted from the universe. Then we'll look at why they became buried and why they've resurfaced relatively recently.

But first, come with me to the fjords and forests of northern Europe to meet the goddesses and gods, giants and monsters that inhabited the land of ice and snow. We will tread the hidden pine-scented paths through the dark mists of Nordic magic and spell-weaving, of the oracle and the user of magic.

Sitting by a fire fragrant with the scent of pine resin and last year's cut wood, we will learn how to cast and use the runes to weave magical spells and divine the future and the energetic resonance around us.

This stepping back to feel the roots of the past has great power.

Part I

THE MAGIC OF THE ANCIENT NORTH

Chapter 1

The Nordic Tradition

The Nordic tradition is currently enjoying a resurgence as more people than ever are trying to understand their experience of the world and their place in it.

We all have roots in our collective history, roots that spread across time and space. Some wither and die; they compost and their trapped energy is reprocessed. Some flourish and spread. Without good roots, a tree will fall, and it is the same for people. Without good roots, we fall.

The runes, if used and treated with respect and honour, provide a support system and life-navigation tool for those keen to learn more about the ancient power of the Nordic tradition.

The Nordic view of the world

This book is written through the lens of Nordic animism. This is the knowledge and practice of engaging with the gods and spirits that inhabit the landscapes, seasons and history of the north of Europe. It is an expression of the realization that everything has energy – energy in the spiritual and metaphysical sense, not just in the scientific. And everything in the sense of the rocks, the trees, the animals, the people, the water, the earth. *Everything*. This implies that everything should be treated with the respect that we would like for ourselves.

What this means is that while we may eat the deer, or cut the wood, or fish the ocean, it is of utmost importance that we do so with respect. We are part of this energetic world, dependent on the life we take to live, just as that life is dependent on us not destroying it needlessly. The same is true for rocks and the earth. While resilient to change, the very ground we walk on needs us to respect it and not abuse it, and we in turn need the ground to support our crops and our homes.

The idea of deep respect for different energies is a pivotal one. Respecting the animal or plant that dies to feed, clothe or nourish us, and not taking more than our share, allows life to continue.

The same is true, in the ancient Nordic view, for the spiritual beings that inhabit this world, from deities to giants. Respect granted and earned is paid back in the form of magic, blessings and luck.

This interconnectivity of energy is the core of how the runes work. The runic shapes are attracted to the energies that are present. And vice versa: the energies are attracted to the runic shapes. All the energies are interconnected. All the *worlds* are interconnected.

The nine worlds of the ancient north

Fifteen hundred years ago, the Nordic people believed that the world they lived in was one of many – nine, in fact – connected by the world tree, a giant ash called Yggdrasil. Knowing what the worlds are and how they interact helps with grasping the energetic picture of the runes. Here's a list:

- ❖ *Asgard:* a beautiful world of green valleys and towering walls at the top of the tree, where the gods live. Valhalla, the home of the valiant dead, is here.

- ❖ *Vanirheim:* a verdant world full of lush fields and seas full of fish, where the Vanir, the farm gods, live

- ❖ *Midgard:* the world where humans live – Earth

- ❖ *Jotunheim:* a frozen landscape of harsh mountains and ice, where the frost giants live

- ❖ *Muspelheim:* the land of fire, where the fire giants live

- ❖ *Loftalfheim:* the land where the light elves or fairies live

- ❖ *Svartalfheim:* the mountain caves where the *Draegr*, the dark elves or dwarves, live

- ❖ *Helheim:* the land of the dead, a quiet misty place ruled by Hela, the goddess of death

- ❖ *Niflheim:* the land where the dishonourable dead, those who broke oaths, are tormented by a dragon called Nithhogg. This is not a nice place.

The magical beings

The magical beings who inhabit the nine worlds belong to different clans or tribes:

Giants

Giants are the primitive, primal gods. They live in wild places, work primitive brutal magic and are interested in very primal nature-based concepts like fire, ice, water, rock, lightning strike, night and wood. They are generally portrayed as the enemies of the Asir and Vanir (*see below*).

Asir

The Asir are the sky gods. They are interested in quite evolved ideas such as justice, rulership and law. And battle – lots of battle. Refined delicate magic is a thing for them. The fertility goddess Freya and her handmaidens are the supreme mistresses of this magic.

Odin, the god of kings, and Thor, the god of thunder, are the gods of the Asir.

Vanir

The Vanir are the farm gods, the gods who are interested in cycles of nature, farming and fertility. Their magic is to grow and nurture. Frey, the god of fertility, with his giant phallus, and Nordir, the god of the sea, are Vanir.

Elves or alfs

There are two types of elf in Nordic magic:

❖ The *Loftalf*, or light elves, are like fairies. Often radiantly glamorous, they use glamour and distraction to get their needs met.

❖ The *Draegr*, dark elves or dwarves, live underground in Svartalfheim, making all the best bling. I mean super-beautiful jewellery.

These two groups don't feature heavily in rune lore, but I've included them so you've an idea of all the magical beings and energies.

The gods of the north

Just as there are many worlds and beings in the Nordic tradition, so there are many gods in the Nordic pantheon, from the king of the gods and the god of kings, Odin the one-eyed, and his wife, Freya, the goddess of fertility, beauty and bravery, to Frey (remember, phallus), and Gerda, the goddess of the northern lights, and Skadi, the goddess of fierce independence and skiing.

There are more deities than I can list here in a meaningful way. But as we come across them in the runes, I will tell their stories to deepen your understanding of how the world of the north worked.

And so we come to the runes themselves...

The hidden runes

Rune means 'hidden' or 'secret'. Herein lies the power of the runes. There is *much* power in the unknown.

When the All-Father, Odin, king of the gods, god of kings, shamanic healing and war, hanged himself from the world tree, he had to die and be reborn in order to discover this secret. In my own words:

> *Nine days he hangs from Yggdrasil, the world tree.*
> *Wounded, pierced by a spear*
> *In agony, fasting, a sacrifice from himself to himself,*
> *Denied food or water.*
> *To obtain the power of the runes.*

More on that later, but it was good news for us: because of Odin's self-sacrifice, we don't have to hang from a tree for nine days to obtain the power of the runes, which I'm sure you'll agree is a win by anyone's measure.

Though the true meaning of the runes has always been secret, known only to a few, their mundane use in writing your name or the names of your ancestors on stone was widespread. A Viking warrior even carved 'Halfdan woz ere' in runes in the ancient Hagia Sophia temple in Istanbul. Countless swords, combs, bits of bone and wood have been found bearing runic inscriptions. Some are simply 'Made by Ulfbuet', while others, shrouded in mystery and the heady aroma of sacred herbs, have much deeper power. These runic sticks, spells inscribed on wood or bone, were used for healing, love and battle – for Nordic magic.

Chapter 2

Nordic Magic

Within the realms of the Nordic energetic cosmos there are many different concepts, some strange to the modern mind. A basic understanding of them will aid you on your adventure into the runes.

Magical concepts of the Nordic tradition

Wyrd

Fate, destiny, doom. Woven by the Norns, the three goddesses at the root of the world tree. This fate is not as prescribed as the Graeco-Roman fate, it's more of a guideline that we can influence, especially with the runes. Yes, the *Wyrd* can grab us and we can find ourselves in a totally unexpected experience. But it is consensual, so we have to choose to go with what the Norns want. They tend to want us to grow and experience new things.

Ond

The Nordic version of *chi* or *prana* – the energy that flows around, through and with us. When we eat yummy food and feel powerful, *Ond* is that energy. When we buzz after a great experience... *Ond*. When its Tuesday afternoon and all we want to do is sit on the sofa and eat pizza... lack of *Ond*.

Hamingja (hai-ming-ya)

Luck or fortune. It's more a community-gathered and -gained energy than an individual one. When we are an effective part of our community and our community supports us, our luck/fortune rises. It's a bit like what is said in *The Secret*: do good, get good.

Magic and energy work in the far north

There is not a lot of evidence for how magic or energy work was practised back in the ancient Nordic day, as most of the sources were corrupted by Christian monks on a mission to convert all the pagans. No blame here – it was what it was.

What we do know is that there were at least two sorts of magic: *Seiðr* and *Galdur*.

Seiðr (see-du-urrr)

Seiðr in Old Norse, Sithur or Sidur in the anglicized version, literally 'rope-making', is the 'classical magic' that we may recognize, the magic of divination, healing and spell-casting. This form of magic was practical, useful every day.

There are several reasons for the name. The first is that women would practise it while weaving the thread for clothes, sails and other fabric. The women of the Dark Ages made the cloth that everyone wore, which meant that everyone had the magic of the matriarch and the women of the house to keep them safe and healthy.

So, the man going off to war would have protection woven into his tunic, the bride would have the magic of love and fertility in her dress, the shepherd would have the magic of sheep-finding and navigation in his cloak. Sithur was used everywhere in ancient Nordic life.

In these times, women owned everything to do with the home – buildings, tools, animals, slaves, the lot. Men owned their bling and their weapons. While not a matriarchal society, it was pretty close. Fighting and leadership were masculine; making life work, feminine. In some ways it was more subtle than that, but this rune book is not the place to expand on it.

Galdur

The other sort of magic, *Galdur*, was sung magic – the ability to sing or chant energy from the *Wyrd* into the magic you wanted it to be. Or, to translate it in a different way, to throw that magic at another.

In old Nordic times, the ability to throw words at someone was super important culturally. It was used mundanely to entertain with riddles and songs and to insult in clever and inventive ways. There is even a legend of Odin teasing Thor in this way. It is showing mastery of not only the physical, but also the magical nature of the words. Wrapping words around the person being sung/chanted at allows the energy of the words to surround them. So it is a way of manipulating reality.

With *Galdur* and Sithur, the basic skills are identical. But while Sithur is commonly practised, you'd go for *Galdur* when you wanted something more specialized. *Galdur* is the specialist magic that is used to do specific jobs.

There are lots of modern examples of sung *Galdur*. You can find some in the Resources at the back of the book. The most developed is by a group called Wardruna. I suggest you check them out. Probably not while driving. The first time I listened to them, I was so taken with the magic, I drove into a bush.

For those of you out there who are music geeks, or even just interested, *Galdur* is sung on a pentamic meter, with instruments such as the tagelharpa, jouhikko or lyre tuned to the singer's voice.

Sithur and *Galdur* are essentially the same magic, practised in different ways – one woven into fabric, the other sung. They could be practised at the same time:

women would sing their magic into the thread that clothed their household or made the sails for a ship.

The magic of the runes

In themselves, the runes are not magic; they are phonetic, a way of writing sounds down. The magic comes when we connect with the resonance of the energy they attract. This energy is there, regardless of our perception of it. The runes are like energetic magnets that are attracted to certain vibrations of the cosmos.

So, the runes are how we can see what fate has in store for us and how we can attract specific energies to our personal *Wyrd*. They are the tools with which we can pluck the individual threads of the *Wyrd* to influence the cosmos the way we want. They act as anchors to bring that magic into the physical. When a spell is created, the runes anchor it to the now, so its effect can be ongoing.

Context is all in this energetic environment. This is one of the key things with rune work in this tradition. When we want to heal using a rune that is typically aggressive, that may mean that our healing is aggressive, like radiotherapy, or a surgeon's knife. If we use a softer runic energy in an aggressive context, that softness can move from a gentle stream to a raging Arctic storm.

Essentially, runes are access points to cosmic energy. We choose how we want to access that energy, and in what context. We can wear a rune as a pendant, or, if we'd like a reminder of how to receive it, draw it with a marker pen on the palm of our hand. We can mark an item with a rune, any rune, and set our intention. If we're marking Berkanan on our phone, for example, we may say out loud: 'I mark this phone with the rune Berkanan to remind me of my resilience.'

Pulling the threads of the Wyrd

The Norns are the three goddesses who sit at the bottom of the world tree, Yggdrasil, and spin the very fabric of the universe into reality. Their names are Urðr (Fate), Verðandi (The Now) and Skuld (What Will Happen). They weave the threads of universal energy into the complex quilt that is life, the universe and everything.

So, the *Wyrd* could be pictured as a shirt made up of millions of threads, each subtly influenced by those around it. Take a look at your jumper, shirt or PJs (whatever you've got on). Look at the threads that have been woven together to make your garment. This is a micro-representation of the *Wyrd* – lots of threads of fate, destiny, will and every other kind of energy you can think of.

Now I invite you to imagine, if you will, what happens if you have a loose thread and you pull that thread. See where the threads around it become tight or loose, pucker up or flail away? This is what the *Wyrd* looks like.

Every time we make a decision, that decision influences the threads around us.

For example, while dressed as a Viking at one early-spring celebration at an ancient farm near me, making runes and runic inscriptions, I met a witchy woman who had a blog. She was there with her kids and said her friend would love me. She then went and told her friend about me. The friend went on to do her own spell, and six months later we met on a beach, independent of the first woman. And I married the woman I met on the beach.

A thread pulled in a field up a hill led to me getting married... This is an example of the *Wyrd*. And one I particularly enjoy.

Imagine now, if you will, what would happen if you could bring all the threads of a similar vibration towards you. What could you influence? What would happen if you could bring all the energy of courage to you? Or all the energy of sex? Or honour? How would that manifest in your world? This is how runic spells (of which more later) influence the *Wyrd*.

When we allow the runes to be influenced solely by the energies around them, without our bias, then we can begin to use them for divination, in a similar way to the Tarot or oracle cards.

In the historical north, the women had the power to divine the fates. Such a woman was known as a *Völva* – a seer, an oracle, a witch.

The oracle: the Völva

In the Viking culture, women owned everything to do with the home, money and farming. As we have just seen, they also spun the fabric, and when they spun, they sang, they worked magic and formed the *Wyrd* into the clothes that everyone wore. This is part of the reason why it was the women who held the magic in the north. Odin wanted that power, and to get it he had to bleed all over the world tree for nine days... Does this give you a hint of another aspect of the magical power of women in Norse society?

The *Völva* was a specialist who held the fates of her village, her people, in her hands, and the women of the village would come to her for healing. Plus, they would send their men to her when they needed more healing/magic than they could provide.

She would probably specialize in one or two forms of *Galdur*, while also being expert in the general Sithur.

To have victory over the energy she was trying to influence, she would have to demonstrate her expertise not only to the people involved, but also to the energies of the runes themselves.

Carving runes into sticks, usually of fruit wood, allowed the *Völva* to see what runic energies were present in the *Wyrd* at that moment. This was done by ritually casting the runes. We'll come to that later, but first let me introduce you to the runes themselves...

Part II

THE RUNES

Chapter 3

Words, Sounds and Meanings

Words

Back in the day, the runes were a means of communication. They were written on swords to show to whom they belonged or by whom they had been made. They were carved on rocks in commemoration of great people. Some were even graffitied in a Christian church by a bored warrior called Halfdan.

Sounds

Runes are sounds more than they are letters. What do they sound like?

Rune	Rune name	Transliteration	Rune sound
ᚠ	Fehu	F	eff
ᚢ	Uruz	U	uh, you

Rune	Rune name	Transliteration	Rune sound
þ	Thurizaz	Th	th
ᚠ	Ansuz	A	ay
ᚱ	Raido	R	rh, arrr
‹	Kenaz	K (C)	cuh
Χ	Gebo	G	guh
ᚹ	Wunjo	W	wuh
ᚺ	Hagalaz	H	huh
ᚾ	Nauthiz	N	en
ᛁ	Isaz	I	eye, ih
ᛃ	Jera	J	yh
ᛇ	Eihwaz	Ï (Æ)	yuh, why
ᛈ	Peroth	P	puh
ᛉ	Algiz	Z/X	ks, ix
ᛋ	Sowolio	S	esss
ᛏ	Tiwaz	T	tuh
ᛒ	Berkanan	B	buh
ᛖ	Ehwaz	E	eh
ᛗ	Mannaz	M	muh, ma
ᛚ	Laguz	L	luh
◇	Ingwaz	Ing	ing

Rune	Rune name	Transliteration	Rune sound
ᛟ	Othala	O	oh, oo
ᛞ	Dagaz	D	dee, duh

As you can see, there are several sounds that we have in modern English that don't exist in the runes. These sounds came from Latin: the 'cu-wu' sound that we represent with 'q'; the 'see' with a harsh vibration that we represent with 'z'; the 'ecs' noise we represent with 'x'. Old Norse did not have these sounds.

Meanings

Here I've provided you with the runes, in order – the order of the poems that were written about them – along with their meanings as I've learned them, taught them and adapted them to the world we live in today. My version of a journey may be different from yours, but I suggest, quite strongly, that you go with my ideas first. Get used to the concepts and see how they fit with you. Get grounded, get strong, and then add your own flavour and texture to the runes.

That's actually one of the most awesome and powerful things about them: you can put your own personal take on them and you can adapt and flavour them in any way that suits you. For example, Fehu. What are wealth and resources to you? I've given you the idea of having enough to share. Perhaps your idea is being on a billboard on Times Square, starring in movies and living in Beverly Hills. Your version is as valid as mine, but start with mine and then add yours when you have what feels like a good solid grounding.

Names

Our personal names tend to have meanings, and it can be fun to find the corresponding runes. For example:

Richard = 'Ric – Hard', meaning 'noble and strong' (good name, right?)

The runes I would associate with those ideas are noble Ingwaz and strong Uruz.

'Lisa' comes from Hebrew, meaning 'God is my oath.' 'God' could be Ansuz and 'oath' could be Tiwaz.

'Emily' means 'hard-working'. 'Hard' could be 'determined', so Eihwaz, and 'working' could be Ehwaz.

In this way, you can build up a *Cenning*, an understanding, of what a name means and then build a runically magical energetic resonance for yourself or your friends and loved ones.

This is a mind game as much as a magical practice, and as the meanings may not be apparent straight away, you can play with them until you feel good with the energies. Then you have your friends' names in runes.

To go the extra mile, you could make those runes into a bind rune for them (*see p.204*), as a gift.

Aettir (et-tear) – rune families

Family and community are big parts of the ancient Nordic mindset, which has huge amounts of interdependence between people. This interdependence, and the need to tell stories about everything, bring the concept of *Aettir* into the runic universe. *Aettir* means 'families', and the runes are in three families of eight runes. This is not an original early medieval construct, but one that was applied later, for example by David and Julia Line, in *Fortune Telling by Runes* in the 1980s.

The runic *Aettir* tell a story, and our Nordic ancestors loved a story. The story of the runes isn't a story like that of the Tarot, which has a very clear and defined narrative, it's much more about the evolution of ideas. The *Aettir* can be seen as a journey of life:

- ❖ The first *Aett* represents the individual, starting with resources (Fehu) and ending with joy (Wunjo).

- ❖ The second *Aett* is how the individual is tested, weathers the storm and can grow and develop, starting with change (Hagalaz) and ending with the sun (Sowolio).

- ❖ The third and final *Aett* is how the individual becomes part of society, starting with duty and honour (Tiwaz) and ending with initiation and passing through the doorway (Dagaz).

The runes as energy

Now, on to the individual runes.

There are three stages to each of the descriptions that follow:

❖ The first section is the basics of the rune, so you can go straight there to see what it's about. This includes information for when you are doing readings, challenges, gifts and inspirations.

❖ Then into the detail: ancient poems, modern uses and how to work with the rune.

❖ Finally, there is an affirmation you can use to connect to that rune.

Runic energy will make itself known in interesting ways. As you learn the runes, you may notice their shapes in clouds, roots or structures around you. This is the energy of the *Wyrd* at work, making you aware of a change in your own energy. You may be working on a spreadsheet and see a runic shape in your coffee, or find the paper clips have fallen in just such a way. This is the universe drawing your attention to where there may be a lack in resources or the scope to expand them.

Be open and willing to take advantage of opportunities that present themselves to you and pay extra attention to your thoughts and dreams, as this is how the *Wyrd* will communicate with you.

FEHU

Fee-Huo

Sound

The 'eff' in 'fire', 'for' and 'fish'.

Inspiration

How can I adapt to increase my resources?

Gift

Abundance.

Challenge

Over-stretched or absent resources.

Old rune text

This old Saxon text tells the story of the rune Fehu:

> Feoh byþ frofur fira gehwylcum;
> sceal ðeah manna gehwylc miclun hyt dælan
> gif he wile for drihtne domes hleotan.

> *Wealth is a comfort to all men;*
> *it must be freely given by every man,*
> *if honour he wishes to gain in the sight of his*
> *lord.*

In *Audhumla*, the creation story of the north, the first cow was formed from the first melt of ice. She provided sustenance for the first gods that she licked from salt. The rune Fehu represents this ability to feed everyone from the cow. In Old Norse, *Fehu* meant 'cattle', and cattle meant cash. The ability to feed your family from your cow was a powerful thing. Cheese and milk were important sustenance.

The Saxon text talks of wealth freely being given. Now, to a pre-industrial society like the Norse, wealth involved being able to rely on your neighbours and to trust someone's word. Reputation was everything. In the Dark Ages, if you had a good reputation, people would speak well of you, feed you on your travels and help you on your way.

Fehu here and now

We see the rune Fehu in modern words like 'feed', 'fee' and 'fed'. It's having money in our bank account and buying our broke friend a meal. It's food for thought, it's paying a fee, it's our boss offering us overtime to make sure we can pay our bills easily this month. It's investing money in an idea and that idea paying us back tenfold (if perhaps not *exactly* how we expected it to). It's buying from small independent businesses rather than multinationals, so that wealth is more evenly distributed within our community.

While people may no longer sing songs about our reputation, when we're a good person who does good things, when we're a person who makes money and shares their wealth and supports others, we are rewarded. We feel good and, as the law of karma – *Hamingja* in Norse – dictates, we get what we give.

Support others and you too will be supported.

Building a relationship with Fehu

Here are a few ways of interacting with the energy of Fehu:

❖ *Celebrate your good deeds:* Back in the day, reputation was spread through songs and oaths and boasts. Now, boasting about how good we are may be perceived as egotistical. Whether you agree or disagree, making a list of all the good deeds you are doing as you go through your day will not only act as a feel-good reminder to your heart and mind, it will be a celebration of the good you have done.

❖ *Serve with no expectation:* When you serve another person, be it a lover, child, friend or family member, do so with no expectation other than to serve.

Fehu will bring that energy back to you; maybe not straight away – remember, it takes time to raise cows – but it *will* come back to you. There is a caveat here – if your contribution is not recognized or acknowledged, then this is an environment that is not ready to receive your energy. If it's all take and no give, then this is a toxic environment for the energy of Fehu, and it's a sign that it's time for you to move on, like the reindeer or aurochs, to new pastures that *will* feed you.

* *Attract wealth:* Place the Fehu rune in your wallet or purse to attract money. Don't name your long-term bank account Fehu, though, as the idea is to attract wealth and to keep it in movement, not hoarded, so make sure you spend money, donate to charity and keep your wealth in circulation.

* *Share food with others:* Make food for a friend who is struggling, perhaps because they've just had a baby, are ill or are experiencing financial difficulties. Make and share something nourishing that they will appreciate. The act of moving your energy from internal to external changes the runic power within you in a way that will allow you to attract more wealth and resources so you can be of more service.

As you delve into your relationship with Fehu, your relationship with your finances, resources and energetic flow will be heightened in every way.

When Fehu shows up

❖ Are you being nudged not to hoard your wealth?

❖ What could you do to expand your wealth?

❖ Check your reputation. What's going on there?

When Fehu appears in a rune cast, it implies that wealth and a good reputation are available and that you need to take action in order to attract them. There's a good chance you'll have to work for them, like those who went before. Fehu does not come to those who sit idle.

Let's go back to the cows. When a herd of cows are allowed to move freely, with access to nourishment, they grow strong. If kept in one place, without sustenance, they sicken and die.

So, if Fehu shows up in the context of your wealth or resources, you're being nudged to make sure there is flow, so that they can grow. There's nothing wrong with holding on to resources to keep yourself safe in times of strife and uncertainty. But if untended, they will not grow, expand or adapt.

When Fehu comes up in a cast, it's also an invitation to expand your wealth. Where can you find new places for your energy, your resources, your money to flow into? Could you choose to buy your coffee from an indie shop rather than from a chain? Could you buy an inspiring piece of art from an upcoming artist? Or are you being encouraged to take a new direction in your work or business? Where can there be movement and flow in your wealth and resources? Where is there a current restriction?

This can apply to your reputation, too. Where are you feeling restricted in your own personal growth? Where are you holding back, not expressing your potential? Fehu here implies that there is the possibility of enhancing how others see you or that you may be stuck in a situation that is not serving you.

Fehu meditation

If you're feeling drained, worn out or that you're running on empty, meditating on Fehu will help to restore your energetic resources.

- ❖ Draw the rune on your non-dominant palm with a sharpie.

- ❖ Then either cover one eye with it, Odin style, or place it on your forehead or over your heart. Head for inspiration, eye for wisdom, heart for knowing.

- ❖ Settle into a comfortable position. I like sitting cross-legged on the floor with a cushion underneath me.

- ❖ Burn some amber essence and focus on your breath. Breathe in through your nose for seven seconds and out through your nose for seven seconds, keeping the image of Fehu in your mind's eye.

- ❖ Do this for between three and six minutes. I use a timer on my phone.

❖ When you've completed this, grab your journal and write down the first 10 ideas, words or concepts that come to you. You may choose to draw, sketch, write – just do whatever feels good to you and gets your ideas out onto the paper. This can give you insight and guidance into both the rune and your relationship with its themes.

Affirmation

'When I share what I have, I become wealthier.'

URUZ

Urr-Uhzz

Sound
The 'uh' in 'thug' or 'slug' and the 'oo' in 'ruse' or 'ooze'.

Inspiration
Where can raw strength and power help here?

Gift
Power, strength, personal responsibility.

Challenge
Physical weakness or misused strength.

Old rune poem
Ur byþ anmod ond oferhyrned, felafrecne deor,

feohteþ mid hornum mære morstapa;

þæt is modig wuht.

The aurochs is proud and has great horns;

it is a very savage beast and fights with its horns;

a great ranger of the moors, it is a creature of mettle.

Uruz is the power, the raw strength of the universe. During Viking times, the most powerful thing they could imagine was the aurochs, a gigantic creature that had massive horns that could gut a man and swing him around its mighty head. It was a prehistoric bison, and you know how big bison are, right? Aurochs made them look small. If you look at the rune, it looks like an aurochs, or ox, with its high shoulders and sloped back.

Like the aurochs, Uruz is powerful and strong. It's mobile power. You can look on it in modern terms as a bulldozer or digger, a huge power that moves, pushing all before it, and, by being big, strong and mobile, it is free and untameable. Uruz represents wild power. Not mad and unpredictable power, like that of a rabid dog, but focused power. It knows where it wants to go and only uses what it needs to get there.

This rune brings forward the energy of your inner power, your Ond, the fierce and fortifying force that sustains and heals you. To channel your Ond is to heal yourself, and Uruz is a great ally in this.

Wild freedom was an important concept to the ancient Vikings. Uruz embodies the energy of the lone warrior setting out on an adventure, or the ship full of intrepid explorers leaving familiar shores to cross unknown seas in search of new worlds. It's having the freedom to do what you need to do, but also taking responsibility for your actions within that freedom. It's no one's fault but your own if your longship falls off the edge of the world or Jörmungandr, the world serpent, eats you.

The energy of Uruz is the masculine life-force, striving to overcome all obstacles and survive all dangers, to adapt to new challenges, to recover from wounding and rebuild power from weakness. Because of this, Uruz is robust, able to weather the storm. It is power, energy and the will to go forward. Regardless of any obstacles.

Uruz is also a powerful energy of self-reliance and self-control. The aurochs could quite literally squish most predators, even wolves, and humans would only approach it in numbers. Uruz is similarly unassailable, confident and hard to stop.

This rune is the essence of stubborn determination.

Uruz here and now
There are several aspects to Uruz in the here and now. In personal, physical terms, it is the strong man. Think Halfthor Bjornson. Uruz is the robust physique that withstands infection or illness.

It is also the power of the freight train, the bulldozer – all but unstoppable as it moves forward with purpose. Where Fehu was the domesticated cow, Uruz is the feral aurochs.

In today's society, self-reliance is a powerful energy. Being able to see where your weaknesses are and ensure that you are resilient and able to defend yourself, as well as stick to your moral path when all around you are wavering, is a powerful gift of Uruz.

Building a relationship with Uruz

You bring this runic energy into your world when you do the following:

❖ *Access strength:* Uruz is your friend when you need the strength to get things done. Use it when you need raw primal power. Put it on your weight gloves or wrist wraps before a big deadlift or squat.

❖ *Embrace the wild:* Exercise more, lift heavy, work out, go walking in nature. Be active.

❖ *Practise healing:* Uruz can bring energy to a person who needs healing. Trace it onto the chest of someone undergoing bone marrow treatments or suffering from an energy-limiting disease like chronic fatigue. Draw it on a dressing, a band aid or a bandage to encourage a wound to heal faster. Write it on a plaster cast to help a limb heal.

- *Push past obstacles:* It's great to use Uruz when you need to push past obstacles, both mentally and physically, including your own patterns, the ones that get in your way or sidetrack you. Uruz likes simple straight lines and isn't very good at being distracted. If you are doing a task that needs will-power, then it is your friend. Beware, though, if that task is in any way delicate or fragile.

- *Ignore criticism:* When you use Uruz for self-reliance, you can expect the barbs and jibes of ill-wishers to simply bounce off you. Aurochs could be shot full of arrows and not mind.

- *Fortify other runes:* Uruz can be used to fortify other runes to produce healing effects, overcome weaknesses, boost confidence and promote continued good health and energy.

When Uruz shows up

- Where is the strength?

- Where is the power?

- Is there stubbornness here? Is it beneficial?

- How is the primal energy manifest?

When Uruz shows up in a rune cast, it brings the idea of strength. Of power. It indicates that power and strength are either present or required. Depending on the question, you will know which thread of the *Wyrd* the rune has attached itself to.

Uruz doesn't just signify physical strength or power, it signifies power in all its forms – psychological, magical, political or any other form you can imagine. It shows power that is running so strongly that nothing can stop it.

The reverse is also true of Uruz in a reading: a lack of power or strength or fortitude can be indicated. Again, depending on the context, Uruz can imply a power vacuum, or not enough strength or will being brought to a situation.

When Uruz shows up randomly in your world, it can be there to throw off unwanted control, break restrictive bonds and take down barriers. It evokes self-reliance, confidence, courage and bravery. It may mean that you need to restore hope and apply some willpower.

As a solution to a problem, Uruz showing up is a sign that your body requires more protein and strength.

Uruz case study

I did a reading for a client, Sarah, who wanted to know how to approach a situation with her boss regarding pay. She'd been overlooked for promotion and had extra work dumped on her. Understandably, she wasn't impressed with this turn of events. No extra money, and then extra work...

In the rune cast, Uruz showed up in the recent past. This implied that she hadn't had enough power to make events happen the way she wanted.

To remedy this lack of power, I set Sarah the homework of saying 'no' to someone at work once a day. That would build an inner pathway that would allow Uruz to support her power of self-determination.

Within six months, she had a bigger promotion, more pay... and a new tattoo of Uruz.

Uruz meditation

When you need some power, some strength in your world, then this Uruz meditation is for you. Doing this in a group is exponential: it doubles your *Ond* for each person doing it with you. So two of you is double, four is eight times, and so on.

This may be a sweaty one, so find your leggings or sweats. You'll also need something that doesn't slip, like a yoga mat.

❖ Draw the Uruz rune on a piece of paper and write 'I am strong' three times in your journal. Keep that idea in your mind

❖ Set a timer for three minutes.

❖ Get down on your hands and knees on your mat. Dig your toes in and almost straighten your legs. Make sure your arms are long and strong, with your fingers pointing forward. Your head can fall between your shoulders.

❖ Roll your shoulder blades open, as if trying to take your biceps into the sky. Imagine you look like the rune Uruz.

❖ The yogi in you will recognize Downward Dog.

❖ As you exhale, chant 'Uruz.' Do this for three minutes. Or, if you're not a masochist, as long as you can. The longer you do it, the more physical strength and mental fortitude you build.

❖ When you've finished, take some time in stillness, lying on your back or sitting comfortably, and journal what you felt. Then make sure you ground your energy by eating something. Chocolate is good.

Affirmation

'I have all the strength I need within me.'

THURIZAZ

Thur-ee-sarz

Sound
The 'th' in 'Thor' or 'thermal'.

Inspiration
Where can focus and single-mindedness help me here?

Gift
Focused strength, piercing insight, direct action.

Challenge
Blind rage, anger, loss of focus, random action.

Old rune poem
> *Ðorn byþ ðearle scearp; ðegna gehwylcum anfeng ys yfyl,*
> *ungemetum reþe*
> *manna gehwelcum, ðe him mid resteð*

> *Thorn is thoroughly sharp, to Lords*
> *Its embrace is evil, endlessly cruel,*
> *no matter what man in the midst of it rests.*

Thurizaz is the thorn. You can see how it got its name simply by looking at its shape. If you've ever found yourself stuck in a bramble patch or thorn bush, or even a cactus patch, you'll know how focused and painful thorns are. They come from all sides and from every direction – focused powerful attacks that are hard to get away from.

This is also the rune of Thor, and is shaped like his hammer, Mjölnir (Moy-lh-ney-huh), Skull-crusher, which he used to defend Asgard's walls and... crush skulls. Weapon names weren't very imaginative back then.

It is also the rune of the giants, or *Thurses* in Old English.

Story time!

The great god Thor is the Nordic god of thunder, lightning and blacksmiths. He is the defender of humankind against all external threats.

In the sagas, there is no bigger threat than the giants. They cause the onset of winter, the growth of the glaciers, the heat in the desert and the fires in the woods. When they get out of hand and cause problems, Thor and his mighty hammer stand ready to protect us.

When Thor was adventuring one day, he was tricked by a giant. One night when he was drinking with the giant by the fire, the giant fell asleep. Thor then decided to smash him in the head with Mjölnir. The giant moved out of the way at the last minute and Thor missed. He brought his hammer down, leaving a massive crater in the ground, and this is how the Ritland Crater in Norway was formed. This just goes to show how powerful this hammer is. When the power of Thurizaz is focused on one spot, it can quite literally create a valley.

The giants, too, are represented by this rune. What do Thor and the giants have in common? They like to fight. Thurizaz could be viewed as a Viking lord in all his armour: massive, hard to kill and the deadliest weapon in existence. Kind of like a modern tank.

One of the best things about Thor is his relentless enthusiasm, and this rune has that in spades. When things get dark and times are hard, Thurizaz is the rune to pull you out of funk and into focused action. Just be sure you're clear on how you choose to focus it.

Thurizaz here and now

Thurizaz is a great rune for the here and now: it is pointy, sharp, focused and adaptable. It is creative masculine energy in action.

The aggressiveness of Thor and the giants is held in the energy of this rune. It attracts defensive powers and can be at the origin of sudden upheavals. It is also a protection rune – not one that hides behind a wall or sets up barriers, but one that thinks the best defence is offence, almost recklessly so.

Thurizaz shows up as 'thorn' in the Anglo-Saxon rune poem, as it is sharp and pointed and can be used to create focus if required. Like a guided missile, its focused destruction can be used like a surgeon's knife to cut out what is unnecessary. To cut away the dross. This pinpoint focus to the exclusion of all else is one of the manifestations of Thurizaz.

It also represents the thorns, the trials of life, the need to fight to reach truth, spiritual knowledge and illumination.

Thurizaz is also a fertility rune in the sense that it breaks down barren, hard, rocky realms into workable soil that brings fruitfulness to crops and wombs.

Building a relationship with Thurizaz

Thurizaz and Uruz both signify power, but whereas Uruz is brute force, Thurizaz is more focused power, like a laser beam. If you were boxing, Thurizaz on your gloves would definitely help. This rune isn't one for nuanced arguments, however. It doesn't work well with distractions; in fact, it ignores them. So don't use this rune in a battle of wits, use it in a battle of fists, or direct action.

The best mental state for working with Thurizaz is enthusiasm, rather than anger or fear, as the former will much better sustain right awareness and diminish the potential danger involved in strong Thurizaz energy.

Use this rune when you want to use focus and direct energy to get things done:

❖ *When going into battle:* While Thurizaz is a rune of protection, don't use it on actual armour, especially helmets, as Thor was hit on the head by a stone that got stuck there – not smart. Thurizaz is of much more use when going into battle – literal or metaphorical – than when seeking protection from harm.

❖ *When you want to be accurate:* Put Thurizaz on your knife sheath or penknife, or indeed anything you want to be accurate with. I have it on my tablet for when I do digital art. I like the accuracy it brings.

❖ *When you need to be focused:* When doing an exam or a task for example, Thurizaz will help you maintain that single-minded focus to achieve your goal.

❖ *When you need to attack from a place of safety:* That may sound super martial; what I mean is if someone is throwing shade at you, Thurizaz will allow you to respond with impunity.

Thurizaz case study

When Simon, a guy who was experiencing problems with staying focused while working from home, approached me looking for help, Thurizaz was the rune that jumped out at me.

Simon put the thorn rune on his laptop and, being an arty graphic designer, he made himself a 'focus' picture that incorporated the rune for his screen wallpaper. This helped him to bring more focus into his life.

When Thurizaz shows up

❖ Who is lacking focus?

❖ Where is power being directed?

❖ Where is cutting energy needed?

❖ How is there piercing energy?

Thurizaz is as pointy as a thorn. In its positive aspect, it implies direct action and focus, with a leaning towards the action. When not used with focus, or not bound by strong morals, however, it does have the potential to be seen as a chaotic and unfortunate rune.

When Thurizaz appears in a reading or shows up in your life, it may represent harmful obsessions, including sexual ones, a bad reaction to a situation or a destructive force, conflict or a changeable nature. It can also signify the will or motivation to change. It can be a warning of impending disruption, but at the same time it can show up as a balancing force helping us to overcome a forthcoming difficulty.

Thurizaz is either chaos or focus – the chaos of unrestrained vital power or the focus of a lightning bolt.

Thurizaz meditation

Find somewhere comfortable, like a sheepskin, or a comfy blanket. If you can sit on your knees with your bottom on your heels, please do so. If that's not comfortable, then place a cushion under your knees and/or bum, or find a sitting position that works for you.

- ❖ Set a timer for three minutes and write in your journal three times: 'I am focus, I am Thurizaz.'

- ❖ Draw Thurizaz on a piece of paper or have the rune stone in front of you.

- ❖ Bring your hands in front of your chest so that your hands grasp your forearms in a monkey grip – make your fingers into hooks, as if you are carrying too-heavy shopping bags, and then hook each hand to the other. Women, have your left palm facing towards your body; men, your right.

- ❖ Start your timer and breathe in through your nose and out of your nose rapidly for three minutes, making lots of noise like a thunderstorm or angry goat. Bringing this thunder energy into your body brings the focus that the thorn brings, as well as the power of the thunder.

❖   When you have finished, write down your thoughts and feelings in your journal.

Affirmation

'I am focused. I am strong.'

ANSUZ

Ahn-sooz

Sound
The 'ay' in 'hay' or 'say' and the 'ah' in 'ash' or 'anchor'.

Inspiration
Where can my acts of ecstasy bring inspiration?

Gift
Inspired communication.

Challenge
Confusion or miscommunication, fake news, manipulation.

Old rune poem
Os byþ ordfruma ælere spræce,
wisdomes wraþu ond witena frofur
and eorla gehwam eadnys ond tohiht.

> **The mouth is the source of all language,**
> **a pillar of wisdom and a comfort to wise men,**
> **a blessing and a joy to every earl.**

This is the rune of the All-Father, Grimnir, Mr Wednesday, Odin. In ancient times, the Norse, Danes, Jutes, Angles and Saxons didn't write *per se*; the mark of a 'literate man', a noble, would be the ability to recount his genealogy to six generations, compose a heroic poem and perform it on the ride home from winning a battle.

Odin and speech

Odin is the god of kings, those who rule and lead. He is aware of his strengths and weaknesses – although the latter are always a little trickier because... well, ego – and he spends his time making sure he is the best he can be: he is the god of self-improvement.

One day he saw that he needed the mead of poetry, a mystical boozy drink made from the blood of a dead god, honey and water (no one said this was a nice story). So he found out where the Draegr, *the trolls, were brewing this essence of poetry and inspiration and headed over there, camouflaged as an eagle.*

When the one-eyed one got to the mountain where the drink was being made, he quickly realized he couldn't get in through the front door, so he found a tiny crack in the mountain that only a worm could sneak through. Being shrewd and clever, he turned himself into a worm and wiggled through the mountain into the chamber where the giant cauldron was bubbling.

Transforming back into himself, he found himself face to face with a beautiful giantess called Gunnlod. Realizing he'd been rumbled, he went into full charm mode and seduced the surprised giantess, who quite frankly found the attention rather flattering after being stuck in a cave for many years.

When she was snoozing and her guard was down, Odin gulped up the contents of the cauldron and smashed his way out of the side of the mountain, holding the liquid in his mouth.

The trolls weren't impressed, and Gunnlod even less so – who wants a lover who steals from you and runs off when you're sleeping? The trolls and the giantess transformed themselves into hawks to follow Odin, who was waddling down the mountainside, his cheeks full.

He saw the pursuit and was afraid. He turned himself into a giant eagle and flew away.

One thing an eagle is not known for is cheek size, and as he flew, Odin dripped drops of the mead of poetry over the entire land, causing humans to become poets, artists and creatives.

When he got home, the other gods stopped the vengeful pursuers and Odin spat his mead into a big jug to keep it for when he needed it.

This is how Odin came to gain the power of poetry and language. And how we humans came to receive divine inspiration from the gods. It's also how we got the rune Ansuz, the rune of words, the tongue and creativity.

Ansuz is the essence of inspiration, communicating with wit and verve, having the wisdom to know when to speak and when to remain silent, when to threaten and when to reconcile. It is the rune of the leader who can inspire great courage and loyalty in their followers and great chagrin and woe in their foes.

So, Ansuz is the Viking embodiment of the fast-talking salesman, the inspirational leader, the double-talking politician and the dexterous therapist – anyone who uses words to get a desired result. Limited only by their ethics.

Ansuz here and now

Wise communication is a great way to see Ansuz. In Saxon, this rune is *Os*, which means 'mouth', and this is where Ansuz helps us speak.

When we meet someone who is charismatic, or we are charismatic ourselves, this is the energy of Ansuz – not charismatic as in beautiful, but engaging and fun to talk to.

Ansuz is the engaging comedian on TV, or the dour newsreader. Ansuz is also the dazzling cult leader or impassioned teacher. Wherever language and words are used, Ansuz is to be found. Language doesn't just have to be words, either – dance and music are also expressions of the energy held here.

Building a relationship with Ansuz

Ansuz is the rune of communication, speech, persuasion and entertainment – things that often trigger fear or anxiety. Use this rune to overcome that anxiety:

- ❖ *When going for an interview or needing to speak with dexterity:* Ansuz is a great rune to put on your PowerPoint presentation, hidden in plain sight to make sure your message gets across and is heard in the way you want it to be.

- ❖ *When seeking creative inspiration:* Stick this rune to your laptop as you write (it's on mine!), paint it on your brushes, draw it on the front of your sketchbook.

❖ *When singing or performing:* Put a sticker or make a mark on your mic and/or your instrument, as Ansuz brings the ability to hold an audience in the palm of your hand, be it with your wit, your voice or your performance.

❖ *When debating:* Add Ansuz to your notes to bring the energy of dexterous words.

When Ansuz shows up

❖ Where is creativity needed?

❖ Where is inspiration lacking, or present?

❖ How is the voice being used?

❖ Why are words being misunderstood?

❖ Who is manipulating the situation?

Ansuz is communication, language, entertainment, song... and manipulation.

When you see this rune, in nature or in man-made structures, be aware of what is being said around you. Is it benevolent? Is it manipulative? *How* it's being said is almost as important as *what* is being said.

Look to technological communication – where are things likely to be miscommunicated? Text messages? Tweets?

Look for hidden messages – what is being covered up? What's *not* being said? Read between the lines.

I've seen Ansuz appear in wires that were leading to a podium for a speaker, and in the rigging for lighting for a speaking gig I was doing. This made me very alert to how I was communicating and what was being said to me.

Ansuz meditation

Ansuz is a great rune for inspiration, for calling in the creative muse. Here's how to do it:

- ❖ Set a three-minute timer.

- ❖ Sit comfortably with your back straight, arms bent, elbows by your sides, hands in front of your chest and palms open and facing away from your body.

- ❖ Now touch the base of your little finger with the thumb of the same hand and bring the base of your thumbs together to create the symbolic wings of Odin's ravens.

- ❖ Breathing in and out through your nose, bring your hands, still in the wing position, to your heart.

- ❖ Bring your focus to the centre of the wings and declare: 'I am open to receive.'

- ❖ Sit in stillness for between two and five minutes.

- ❖ When you have finished, journal what has come through for you.

❖ Then relax for a few minutes, drink some water, embrace your inspiration and create.

Affirmation

'My words are my magic.'

RAIDO

Ray-Do

Sound
'Rh' or 'arr' as in 'ride', 'raid' or the noise a pirate makes.

Inspiration
Going on an adventure, taking risks, trying new things. The thrill of the journey.

Gift
The excitement of new experiences.

Challenge
Too much focus on adventure with no regard for real-life events.

Old rune text
Rad byþ on recyde rinca gehwylcum sefte
ond swiþhwæt, ðamðe sitteþ on ufan meare
mægenheardum ofer milpaþas.

> *Riding seems easy to every warrior while he is indoors, and courageous to him who traverses the high roads on the back of a stout horse.*

In the dim mists of history, your reputation was valuable. Raido is what reputation is built on – adventure; the ability to live life, take risks and gain experiences. It's the thrill of the open road, the excitement of discovering the unknown...

It was part of the psyche of the Nordic clans to actively go and seek adventure. Raido is that call, that yearning, that *need* to see what's over the mountain. Not simply for a change of scenery, but because the yearning for new experiences, for freedom from social norms, is a deep-rooted requirement.

In Viking Age society, the mark of a warrior, a worthy person, was the ability to tell stories of his amazing adventures and to bring news of far-off lands and people. This was a mark of renown.

Raido here and now

It's much the same here and now – if you go travelling, backpacking and exploring, when you come back, you tell your friends and peers all the amazing things you've done, and it builds your reputation. That's Raido. When you step outside your front door into a cold morning, with only streetlights illuminating the mist, and then drive to the airport, that's Raido. When you embark on childbirth for the first time, or set forth on *any* journey into the unknown, or any journey, full stop, you have the same spirit of adventure, because Raido doesn't care where you're going. The important thing is that you are in motion.

The epitome of Raido in modern culture is the biker – the person who packs a bag and simply allows the open road to be their guide. That's Raido – the wind in your hair, and nothing but freedom, opportunity and possibility in front of you.

Raido is not just the journey from A to B, though, it's the spiritual journey. The archetypal hero's journey. It is also a powerful aid in any shamanic or Sithur practice. When you embark on a spiritual quest, remember that you are engaging in what others have done for millennia before you: grow, expand and learn through the quest, the act of embarking on an adventure.

Building a relationship with Raido

There are several ways of inviting travel and adventure into your experience:

◆ Put Raido on your passport or something that you keep super close to you. Don't stick it on your luggage, or your luggage will go travelling on its own, and we all know how frustrating it can be to arrive at a hotel with no change of underwear. Of course, this is the essence of Raido too – a new experience. To be relished. If possible.

❖ Raido is your ally when it comes to taking a journey that is going to be long and boring. Got to drive 10 hours to a wedding in the desert? Then Raido will make it interesting. Be careful how you choose your interesting, though, as Raido is also a blow-out at 60 on the motorway. Remember, you get to create your experience of *any* journey – it can be a 'boring' commute to work or it can be an epic adventure surrounded by people in a metal box, each with their own unique story.

❖ Raido is also your ally when you are meditating or on a shamanic journey. Think of it as a catalyst that makes it easier for you to take a different energetic pathway. Place it on your journal or maybe embroider it on your medicine blanket.

When Raido shows up

❖ Where could a journey take you?

❖ When could you go?

❖ How could you seek adventure?

❖ What could you experience?

❖ Who could help you?

Raido in a reading implies an impending journey or the yearning for one – the spirit of adventure, of freedom.

The challenge that Raido can present is the opposite: the stagnation of inaction. Take note of the context in which it shows up.

If you chance across a representation of Raido while out and about, again check the context. Could it be leading you down a rabbit hole, like Alice, or is it preparing you to make a decision that could see you embracing the experience of being alive and all the adventures that are to come? Don't be afraid to follow the signs that Raido leaves for you, especially if you want an experience to tell your friends about around a warm fire.

Raido meditation

For this meditation you need your journal and a pen, and a timer if you have one.

❖   Draw or write Raido in your journal.

❖   Sit comfortably, or lie down if that suits you better.

❖   Breathe in and out through your nose.

❖   Bring to your mind's eye an image of yourself travelling, as if you were watching yourself in a movie. In fast-forward, watch yourself doing the awesome things you are going to do on your adventure.

❖   When it is over, rerun the video in your mind.

- ❖ Do this every day for at least 21 days to build the energies into your system, so when you go travelling, you will find the adventure you crave.

- ❖ The video you run can be different each time, but make sure it's the same journey. The journey is the same, the adventure differs.

Affirmation

'Adventure offers growth and opportunity.'

KENAZ

Ken-az

Sound

The 'cuh' in 'king', 'cat' or 'catch'.

Inspiration

Illumination in the darkness.

Gift

Insight into the hidden.

Challenge

Blinkered focus, burning heat.

Old rune poem

> *Cen byþ cwicera gehwam, cuþ on fyre blac ond beorhtlic, byrneþ oftust*
> *ðær hi æþelingas inne restaþ.*

> *Torch is obviously fire for each living being,*
> *shining; most often it burns*
> *where the princes rest.*

Kenaz is torchlight shining in darkness. Chasing fear away.

Insight, wisdom and knowledge often only come when we've experienced pain, strife and a fight for survival. This has been the pattern of human evolution. It has been through war, death and plague that we have made great innovative advances. But it's rare that we actively *choose* to look into the darkness, because most of us have been told that it's there that fear resides.

In the north, when you have less than an hour of daylight a day at midwinter, it's important to make sure that you have enough light to see, and be seen, and be safe. So, for the Nordic peoples, shining light into darkness became practically a religion. This form of illumination allowed them to live their lives in the darkness of winter, punctuated by twinkles of radiant light.

The Vikings wore lots of shiny silver jewellery, often set with polished stones and gems and, if they were super rich, gold. Their long halls were lit with oil lamps or rush torches, or the cooking fire. When in a place that is just lit by a single-flame light source, the gleam of silver, gold and gems is greater. They twinkle. Try it tonight – polish up your favourite jewellery, close the curtains and light a candle. See how the light reflects off your jewellery. It even works with steel – not stainless, though.

This rune can also be seen as knowledge or insight chasing the darkness of ignorance away. The Vikings set great store by word and language games. Kenaz is the ability to see through the confusion and solve the riddle.

There is another side to it too. As mentioned earlier, it's often pain that drives innovation and sight. The pain of an ulcer or cancer drives people to look for healing. The pain of the loss of a child can push a quest for meaning. Growth through adversity. Still growth, just not particularly pleasant.

Kenaz here and now
In modern terms, Kenaz is the drive for innovation, the mapping of the genome, the finding of a vaccine, the development of a drug.

This rune is also the truth hidden in the lies. In the world of social media, fake news and mass communication, it is the fact-check, the investigation that seeks the truth that's hidden in the darkness.

Kenaz is also exploratory surgery. It's the researcher looking for new information. Raido wants the adventure, Kenaz wants the knowledge and wisdom that come from it.

When you're searching the internet, your search engine is Kenaz. Just remember what other energies are at play and will potentially affect the outcome. Who has paid to be seen and who is manipulating the results? Kenaz is about seeing both the result you want and the other influences.

A super-powerful use of Kenaz is precognition, the ability to see the future (or hear, feel or smell it, depending on your wiring). Kenaz is a powerful ally in cutting through the mists of the *Wyrd* to see what's ahead.

Building a relationship with Kenaz
Kenaz is the light in the darkness, so:

❖ Draw Kenaz on your Post-its as you learn something new at school, college or work.

❖ Stick it on the inside frame of your glasses to help you find what you need to find.

❖ When looking for something in a shopping centre or mall, draw Kenaz on a piece of paper and put it in your pocket. It will help you to find what it is you're looking for.

❖ It's also great for helping find lost keys. Or any missing thing.

❖ When you are trying to find the truth in a situation, Kenaz will help you sift through the lies and the half-truths. Remember that it likes the truth, no matter what the context or consequence. This rune would happily open Pandora's box just to see what was in it.

❖ Paint/stitch/draw Kenaz on your rune or Tarot pouch to aid you in seeing clearly through the mists of the *Wyrd*.

When Kenaz shows up

❖ Where is the darkness in this situation?

❖ Who is in the darkness? Who is shedding the light?

❖ What is hidden?

❖ Where can the light be most effective?

❖ Why is the darkness causing problems?

Kenaz implies there is something hidden that you need to illuminate. It may have been hidden deliberately. The context of the question will help to find what or where it is.

In a health-related question, Kenaz implies inflammation or something that creates a dull pain, like an ulcer or a growth. Maybe not literally, but figuratively. This inflammation will need to be investigated, as it won't be easy to identify. Kenaz implies that knowledge or enlightenment needs to be searched for.

When you are aren't looking for knowledge or asking about it and Kenaz shows up, keep an eye out, as something may be hiding in plain sight.

Kenaz meditation

Kenaz brings the aura of insight to you. This meditation will help with that energy.

❖ To start, sit comfortably on a chair or sofa, or the floor. Use cushions to make life better.

❖ Grab your journal and draw or write Kenaz on a blank page.

❖ When you are comfortable, focus on the tip of your nose. You can have your eyes open or closed.

❖ Then roll your tongue up, so the tip of your tongue is trying to touch the back of your mouth.

❖ Set the timer and stay in that position for three minutes. Try and keep the image of Kenaz in your mind's eye.

❖ When you have finished, journal anything that came up.

❖ Repeat every day for a week, or when you need to boost your insight.

Affirmation

'I can see what is hidden.'

GEBO

Geeh-Boh

Sound

The 'guh' in 'gift' or 'goat'.

Inspiration

I saw this and thought of you.

Gift

Trust, honour, gifts.

Challenge

Greed, jealousy, resentment.

Old rune poem

> *Gyfu gumena byþ gleng and herenys,*
> *wraþu and wyrþscype and wræcna gehwam*
> *ar and ætwist, ðe byþ oþra leas.*

> *A gift is, for heroes,*
>
> *Not an ornament and dignity that impel their grace,*
>
> *but a support for those with no other.*

Back in the day, wealth was hoarded by those who had the martial/military power to defend it. Those without that strength missed out. This may sound harsh, but there is an important aspect of the culture that rebalanced it to an extent: rulers, jarls and kings all had to give gifts to their followers. So, a lord would give visitors clothes, food and shelter. This showed them that they were valued and showed everyone else that the lord was noble and kind.

In the runes, Fehu is a gift that seeks a return – a service or another gift. Gebo is a gift that expects no return: 'Because I *can* give you something, I *will* give you something.' Gebo is the joy of giving.

It does bring an obligation, though – the obligation to give and the obligation to accept and receive. Trust is required, too: giving a gift from a position of power to an 'inferior' requires the trust that they won't use your gift against you. In Viking times, the 'ring-giver' or lord would not just give gifts of jewellery, but swords, spears, weapons and armour. Often these gifts would become ancestral possessions. Giving a sword or spear to someone who is a trained killer implies that you trust them not to kill you. Trust and respect are part of Gebo.

Gebo here and now
Gebo right now is epitomized by the gift-giving extravaganza that falls around the winter solstice in Christian countries. The act of giving presents to bring cheer in the darkest part of the year is the essence of Gebo energy.

Gebo is also the signing of the contract, the implied trust that comes from signing a mutually beneficial agreement. Where there is no trust, there is no Gebo.

When we give a project energy, focus and trust, we get results. In movies, for example, the hero or heroine works hard to get the skill or ability they want. This exchange of energy, of focus, builds the Gebo energy to allow them to receive what they've been working for. It's the same in real life.

So, Gebo is the great manifester. When you put yourself in a place that allows you to receive gifts, Gebo will get them to you.

Building a relationship with Gebo
There are many ways to do this:

❖ Give gifts because you can – not just random tat, but gifts that mean something to the receiver. This builds the energy of the ring-giver within you.

❖ Put Gebo on a document, presentation, flow chart or mood board to help your desires manifest.

❖ Put Gebo on cards, or labels on packages, or messages to loved ones – but wait, we do that, anyway, right? Kisses at the end of a card or letter? xxx

❖ It's great to incorporate Gebo into designs for websites or business cards so that people will want to trust you. It brings the implication of equal returns and trust.

When Gebo shows up

❖ Why would you give/receive a gift?

❖ Where would the gift come from?

❖ What gift would enhance your reputation?

❖ Who would get the most from the gift?

❖ When would the gift be most appreciated?

In a reading, Gebo suggests that there is an opportunity to build trust and good relationships. Be aware of the context, though, as the challenge of Gebo is jealousy or want. Gebo in a draw can mean either an abundance or a lack of trust.

Basically, Gebo is the energy of exchange of, well, energy. Looking to see where energy can be gifted or used to foster this idea will help to answer the question. Remember everything is energy. Einstein said so.

When you are out on your adventures and you spy Gebo, consider what you can give from this experience. Could you entertain your friends by telling them what happened? Share what you learned with others? Make art that stirs the soul? Give a friend or neighbour who doesn't get out much a lift to see what you've seen? Look for an opportunity to foster trust in your life.

Gebo meditation

As Gebo is the rune of giving, here is an active meditation. Quite simply, when you are out and about, see what gifts you can give.

Good examples are:

- *A postcard:* one that lets someone know you are thinking of them, handwritten and with a stamp. This increases your renown and means something to people.

- *Coffee/tea:* giving a warm drink to someone on a cold day can make all the difference to their world.

- *Time:* Time is super valuable. When you give your time to a cause, you aren't just giving your labour, but what it would cost to employ you. So find somewhere to volunteer your time. Not as a penance, but as a gift.

Gifting increases your energy, especially within the groups to which you give. Use that energy to fuel your creativity.

Affirmation

'I am worthy of receiving.'

WUNJO

Wun-Yo

Sound

The 'wuh' in 'win', 'water', 'wish' or 'Wellington'.

Inspiration

I have all I need.

Gift

Contentment and safety.

Challenge

Longing, fear.

Old rune poem

> Wenne bruceþ, ðe can weana lyt sares
> and sorge and him sylfa hæfþ blæd
> and blysse and eac byrga geniht.

> *Joy never ends for the one who knows little of woes, sores and sorrows.*
>
> *He gets success and bliss and enough in his home.*

In today's society, many people live in luxury that was unimaginable to even kings and emperors 1,000 years ago. Life was hard then – no heating, no running water, no supermarkets. Food had to be hoarded for winter and then made to last to ensure that everyone survived.

Wunjo is when we have all we need to make sure we and our family are safe. Our belly is full, we're wrapped up warmly and our loved one is by our side. That was the goal of the people who lived in the Dark Ages: to be comfortable. And that is the energy of Wunjo: being content with what we have, knowing that it is enough to see us through, knowing that we've got the skills and resources to weather the storm. It's the warm, fuzzy bliss of everything being as it should be.

As a challenge, Wunjo has the potential to be the longing for safety that we have when everything has gone wrong. It's that feeling of yearning, of loss, of pain.

Wunjo here and now

Wunjo is every experience and emotion that we associate with contentment. When we learn a skill that makes our life easier, Wunjo. When we rub our puppy's belly, Wunjo.

In the here and now, Wunjo is sitting on the sofa on the day after we've been paid, with our favourite food in front of us and our favourite programme on TV. Everything is going right and we are warm, safe and secure.

The contented dog on his blanket is the energy of Wunjo, as is the cat asleep on the radiator, as is the Danish concept of *hygge*. If you've ever enjoyed reading a book indoors on a rainy Sunday or a cup of hot cocoa on a snowy day, you've experienced Wunjo.

Wunjo today is enjoying the simple pleasures of life, whatever they are to us.

Building a relationship with Wunjo

It's all about comfort:

❖ *Make a Wunjo nest:* This is the way to build a meaningful relationship with Wunjo. All of your favourite things go into your Wunjo nest, from your favourite scent to soft, cuddly things, to your favourite food and drink, and the cat if you can convince it. Make your nest your very own bliss place. Though you can invite others in if you would like.

❖ *Get cosy:* Putting Wunjo on the label of your favourite pyjamas is a great way to do this. This energy will attract the comfort vibrations of the universe to your PJs.

✦ *Be comfortable when out and about:* Having Wunjo on the inside of your sleeping bag while out camping will bring that energy of contentment while you are snug inside your tent. This is a great environment in which to use Wunjo, as camping can be uncomfortable, especially if you aren't used to it.

✦ In this vein, Wunjo is great to use when travelling. If you are stuck in a coach and all you want is to feel that warm, fuzzy feeling, don't reach for the little bottle of gin, but draw Wunjo on your eye mask or your socks before you board.

When Wunjo shows up

✦ When are you most content?

✦ What do you need to put in place to feel safe?

✦ Who can help you feel content?

✦ Why are you lacking contentment?

✦ What would you like to bring the energy of Wunjo to?

In a reading, Wunjo implies the answer to the question will require an aspect of comfort or relaxation. This could be the way to solve the problem or what will happen when the question is answered.

The challenge of Wunjo will be made evident if the reading implies that there is a painful longing or the desire for comfort in the questioner's world-view.

When Wunjo shows up randomly in the wild, ask yourself where you can bring more cosiness and relaxation into your life. Or where there is a painful longing. If you suspect this, try to ease that longing, as unresolved Wunjo can cause problems.

Wunjo meditation

❖ Set your timer for three minutes, then draw or write Wunjo in your journal.

❖ Sit comfortably, with your back straight. Bring your hands to shoulder level with your elbows at your sides, palms facing each other. Point your index finger up and hold the other fingers down with your thumbs.

❖ Close your eyes and bring Wunjo to your mind's eye.

❖ Breathe in and out through an 'o'-shaped mouth.

❖ After your three minutes, journal anything that came up.

Affirmation

'I am everything I need.'

HAGALAZ

Ha-Ga-Laz

Sound

The 'huh' in 'house', 'horse', 'head' or 'helicopter'.

Inspiration

Change comes. Ride it.

Gift

This too shall pass.

Challenge

Destroy all that is known.

Old rune poem

> *Hægl byþ hwitust corna; hwyrft hit of heofones lyfte,*
>
> *wealcaþ hit windes scura; weorþeþ hit to wætere syððan.*

> *Hail is the whitest grain, it whirls down from the sky's heights,*
> *tossed in the wind shower, becomes water thereafter.*

Hail is a pain. Ask any farmer. It flattens fields and makes the crops unusable. To Viking Age farmers, who had no modern machinery, it wasn't just a pain, it was catastrophic to crops and livestock. In Norway and Iceland, hail comes straight off the Atlantic and has nothing to slow it down or lessen its force. In Scandinavia, it can be huge, like tennis-ball-sized, or heavy, like a hammer blow, or, if you're super unlucky, both. And then it melts away, leaving behind it the destruction, but none of the evidence.

This is what Hagalaz energy attracts – devastating change. That sounds negative, and it may feel that way. The point that Hagalaz makes is that total change can also bring adaptation and new growth. Mainly so that we don't get hurt again.

How we respond to the change dictates how we recover and grow. It may be a case of 'adapt or die'. Ask the dinosaurs about that one. Medical science accelerates in times of strife and hardship, and society evolves when threatened.

The same happened for the ancient people of the north. When conditions changed, they had to change from fishermen to raiders in order to feed their families. And as they came into contact with other peoples, their cultural identity changed. Eventually they adopted their neighbours' social constructs and became Christian. They evolved through strife and change. This is the energy Hagalaz brings.

Hagalaz here and now

In the here and now, Hagalaz is the energy of drastic change due to outside influences. It's the messy break-up that moves you to another city, job and life. It's also the energy of being adult enough to move on with your life and not try to reclaim what once was. There is a new reality, and as a mature person, you've got to adapt and deal with it.

Hagalaz doesn't leave much to come back to, so there's often little choice but to rebuild. The challenge isn't surviving the destruction, it's adapting to the new world after it.

On an intimate level, Hagalaz implies relationships changing. Be they romantic, economic or business, when they're washed away, we get to see how strong and adaptable we are. This is rarely pleasant. I know of no one whose life has been completely changed by a wave of golden Labrador puppies wanting to lick them into multimillionaire-hood.

Medically, sepsis or another whole-body infection is the energy of Hagalaz. This isn't pleasant either.

Hagalaz isn't an evil or vindictive energy, though, it just is. Change happens. How we respond to it is a marker of our power. Hagalaz is also the ability to develop resilience. When that heavy hail falls for the first time, we get a bruise. The second time, we hide. The third time, we teach others to hide as well. This is Hagalaz.

Building a relationship with Hagalaz

Hagalaz isn't something we generally want to involve ourselves in. Who likes to have everything change around them? Especially catastrophically. The part of this energy to focus on is 'This too shall pass.' Hail doesn't last forever.

To build resilience and adaptability:

❖ *Remember Hagalaz isn't malignant or evil.* It has no consciousness to be evil with. It is just change.

❖ *Be prepared.* This is *the* lesson of Hagalaz. Nothing is fixed; everything can change.

❖ *Refuse to be stuck in the now.* Knowing it will pass is super important. This applies to all of the minute Hagalaz experiences we have during the day – the spilt coffee, the cat poop on the slippers, the toddler tantrum in the supermarket. All change the situation around them. All pass, all have to be recovered from, and, if we're lucky, learned from.

When Hagalaz shows up

❖ Sudden change is happening/coming.

❖ Brace yourself for a new experience.

❖ Be ready to adapt and learn.

❖ Remember that challenge breeds growth.

Hagalaz in a reading is much like the Tower card in the Tarot. It means change – quick, aggressive and total change. But not with any particular malice. Be aware of clues hidden in the question that may show you where this change may be found.

Hagalaz implies that there is the *potential* for change as well. This will not be gentle. Other runes bring that energy; this energy is catastrophic, noisy, inconvenient change that gets everywhere. This is like a mud slide, on an Easter weekend, on the West Coast main line, or any other major railway line: everything has to change, travel plans get messed up and we have to learn how to get to our destination in a different way.

If Hagalaz makes itself known as you go about your everyday life, get ready for change. Perhaps practically, like checking your emergency kit or bugout bag is where it should be. Maybe making sure your CV is up to date or that you have the resources you need for a sudden life change. Or simply bracing yourself, as your toddler is about to have a tantrum.

Hagalaz meditation

This meditation will help you release any Hagalaz energy that may be caught up in your energy pathways.

You'll need a timer, journal, pen and somewhere warm to sit or lie. I do this lying down. If you feel unwell at any time during this meditation, stop straight away. Knowing when to stop is as important as letting go.

❖ Set your timer for three minutes.

❖ Inhale deeply, pushing your tummy out all the way, and then exhale, squishing your tummy all the way in, and then your chest all the way in. Repeat about 20–30 times rapidly. It doesn't matter if you get it wrong a few times.

❖ When you've done enough (a good sign is tingly toes and fingers), exhale all the way out and hold your breath out for as long as you can.

❖ Bring the rune Hagalaz to mind as you lie there in stillness.

❖ When the urge to breathe gets too much, breathe in, hold your breath for 10 seconds and then exhale.

❖ You can do this as a one-off, or up to five times in a row.

❖ Journal anything that came up for you.

Affirmation

*'I am able to change and adapt
with the situation.'*

NAUTHIZ

Naou-TH-iz

Sound

The 'en' in 'need', 'naughty', 'nose' and 'nubbin'.

Inspiration

The will to survive.

Gift

Tenacity.

Challenge

The crush of defeat.

Old rune poem

> *Nyd byþ nearu on breostan;*
>
> *weorþeþ hi þeah oft niþa bearnum to helpe and to hæle gehwæþre,*
>
> *gif hi his hlystaþ æror.*

Necessity is distress on the chest and often strife of the servant.
It becomes help and healing for the children if they listen soon enough.

Nauthiz quite literally means 'need'. Need in the most primal sense of the word. Humans have three basic needs: air, water and food. When we get those needs met, we are safe – safe for three minutes before we need to breathe again, three days before we need to drink again and three weeks before we need to eat again. Those are extreme numbers, and we tend to breathe 16-ish times a minute, drink a couple of litres of water a day and eat a few times a day too. This stops our body going into survival mode.

The ancient peoples of the north knew need, striving to survive in the frost, trying to till soil that wasn't very fertile. The need of the Vikings pushed them into their longships to seek out new lands.

Nauthiz is this need to survive, to ensure your personal survival and the survival of your bloodline. It is not prospering; it is enduring in order to continue living.

Nauthiz is both individual and collective. A village will only survive when everyone works together to, quite literally, keep the wolf from the door. Individually,

Nauthiz is doing what is right for us personally. These two were rarely exclusive in ancient times.

Nauthiz here and now

Today there's more to our survival than 'just' not freezing to death or ensuring we can eat. The threats aren't as physical as a wolf eating us or extreme weather destroying our crops, but more existential, such as, 'Will I get fired?', 'How do I pay my bills?' and 'What is Steve in Accounts saying about me?'

Society has given us other needs beyond air, water and food. It's given us social acceptance, inclusion and achievement, to name a few. But the energetic pattern coming from the wolf or the hail is the same as the 'Can I afford groceries?' energy.

Whatever the threat, Nauthiz is the super-primitive need to stay alive. It asks the question: 'What do I need in order to survive right now?'

Building a relationship with Nauthiz

You know that first breath of air when you've been stifled? That feeling of freedom when you've just got out of a gnarly relationship? When you don't have to be worried about saying or doing the wrong thing and you can just be yourself?

Nauthiz is the drive that pushes us beyond the stagnant place of fear and into freedom. When we step out of the fear space and into meaningful action, that is Nauthiz.

That being said, Nauthiz is also being curled up in a ball sobbing because we are afraid. 'Choose your fear' is what Nauthiz says. 'Choose action or inaction.'

If we *don't* choose, it's always inaction, and our power is gone. Nauthiz lays out the path to freedom; we have to choose whether to follow it or not. That's how to build a relationship with it.

Remember, Nauthiz isn't focused on avoiding pain or discomfort, just on satisfying needs.

When Nauthiz shows up

❖ Where are your needs not being met?

❖ What do you need in order to move forward?

❖ Where is there a fundamental lack?

❖ What is your general feeling about your situation? What does it need?

When Nauthiz appears in a reading, see where the question implies a need not being met. Nauthiz will indicate the action needed to resolve that. It implies a need to act, be it physically, emotionally or spiritually. Inaction would benefit from being a choice, not a lack of choice.

Nauthiz also represents self-expression and the ability to self-actualize. So, when it shows up, look to where you (as the asker) aren't being true to yourself and your goals.

When you are out adventuring and Nauthiz shows up, be aware of the potential for having to act to guarantee your basic needs are met. Maybe ensure there is a winter kit in your car, or a summer one. Make sure you have water and a snack in your bag if you're off out for the day. Or that you have the right clothes for the environment.

If Nauthiz shows up randomly in your day, look to where your basic needs aren't being met.

Nauthiz meditation

This meditation is one that is challenging, and that I do every day. I don't journal, but I do have the concept in my mind. You can choose to journal if you'd like.

❖ Have a nice warm shower in the morning. Get squeaky clean and then turn the heat off.

❖ Run the shower on cold, initially for 15 seconds and building up to a couple of minutes over a few months.

❖ That breath that comes when the cold water hits your chest or shoulders? That is Nauthiz. The more you experience the shock to the system, the more you will be able to expand your capacity to be alert, tolerant and able to create focused and directed results, and not purely to meet basic needs in the way that our primitive ancestors did.

Affirmation

'I've got this.'

ISAZ

Eees-az

Sound
The long 'eye' in 'ice', 'I' and 'right', and the short 'ih' in 'igloo', 'inglorious' and 'holistic'.

Inspiration
Swift movement.

Gift
Look beneath the surface to find the treasure.

Challenge
Treacherous footing can lead to a shock.

Old rune poem
> *Isa byþ ofer cealdunge metum slidor*
> *glisnaþ glæshluttur gimmum gelicust*
> *flor forste geworuht fæger ansyne*

> *Ice is mightily cold and slippery.*
> *It shines like clear glass, like jewels.*
> *Land worked upon by cold is beautiful to look at.*

Isaz is the rune of ice, frost and frozen things. Back in the Dark Ages of Scandinavia, ice was a real problem. When the sun doesn't shine, and snow and ice build up, ice can quite literally kill you.

Isaz resonates with both the beauty of the frozen landscape and the threat that comes from it. Frozen rivers provide easy ways to navigate snow-covered land, making travel even faster than during the summer. This is part of Isaz – the ability to use ice to move quickly. There is a threat, though – what if the ice isn't thick enough and it cracks? The glittering roadway gives way to an icy tomb...

Isaz also allows for ice fishing, but this isn't without risk either. The hunter finds fish that would otherwise be inaccessible by digging a big hole in the ice, but again, what if the ice were to crack?

The rune poem speaks of the beauty of ice, of how it shines like jewels. These jewels dissolve when the sun comes, so Isaz brings the energy of temporary beauty that is as mysterious as it is fleeting. Ice comes and goes, ebbs and flows.

It has power, though. The glaciers that created the fjords across Scandinavia and Antarctica were formed from ice. It has the power to grind down mountains. Isaz has this power too: if left unchecked, it can, over time, radically change everything around it.

Isaz is one of the core energies of the Nordic tradition, illustrating the belief that the world is harsh and cold and hostile, but can change. Every rune has Isaz in it, bringing that energy to it. The rune itself is a vertical line, and all of the other runes have straight lines in them.

Isaz here and now

Today, Isaz has a very similar energy. Ice has not changed. In the UK, the whole country stops when conditions are icy. It's the same in Texas. Just by existing, Isaz disrupts life. It forces us to adapt.

But by stopping growth, Isaz does bring opportunities. The freezer compartment is a great example of this. It can stop food going bad by stopping all growth, allowing us to have a mango smoothie even in the coldest winter.

Isaz also allows for smooth movement over rough terrain – ever seen *Ice Road Truckers*? – but this swift movement doesn't come without a risk. We may travel swiftly via paths we could not normally take, but we risk plunging into inky depths.

The glittering brightness that is ice can also dazzle, distract and mystify. Snow glare is a real problem, so much so that to stop it the ancient Saami and Inuit developed special glasses made from whalebone before glasses were invented.

Isaz freezes everything. When we freeze, the things that no longer matter fall away and only what is true remains. This is a psychological trait that mammals have. We freeze when we are overwhelmed, which allows us to drop all that is not needed and simply to be with what is.

Building a relationship with Isaz

A relationship with Isaz is one wrapped in brittle glass-like fragments that glitter and then melt away with the sun. To build it:

❖ *Foster swiftness and glamour:* Look to where you can use your sense of self to foster either swift movement or glittering, fleeting glamour.

❖ *Reduce friction:* You can use the energy of Isaz to glide smoothly over things that could potentially be abrasive. This isn't to say you'll avoid having to deal with the abrasiveness, but you can slide over it for now.

❖ *See clearly:* Use Isaz energy to help remove the glamour of self-delusion. Or any glittering distraction that isn't part of the real you.

❖ *See another path:* When you don't want to be where you are, but the way forward isn't clear, Isaz can show you another path. This will, however, probably be temporary and fraught with pitfalls and dangers. You'll get what you need, but is the risk worth it?

When Isaz shows up

✦ What is confusing you?

✦ Is there a glamorous distraction?

✦ What is locked solid and needs to move?

✦ What is moving and needs to be solid?

Isaz is one of those energies that could potentially show up all over the place, and if you chose, you could see it everywhere. Perhaps a better idea would be to take note when things happen with the energy of Isaz. When you discover the energy, then you can look for the rune.

Isaz wild in the world means that there is 'glamour' present, that someone or something has put up a façade, and that you can choose to see that façade or let it melt. It could be yours, it could be another person's or it could be something that people want you to believe.

A wild Isaz can also mean that you need to check your path before you move forward. Could there be hidden pitfalls or hazardous surfaces?

Isaz in a reading often means that adjacent energies can flow easily from one to another. What I mean by this is that if you have runes on either side of the Isaz rune, their energies can potentially merge.

For example:

- ❖ Past: Uruz (Strength)
- ❖ Present: Isaz
- ❖ Future: Tiwaz (Honour)

Here, the energy from past and present and present and future are merging, implying that strength and honour are needed in the present.

Isaz in a reading can also mean that there is something hidden beneath the surface or that should be avoided or circumvented. So be aware of hidden challenges moving forward.

Isaz meditation

This meditation will bring the energetic benefits of Isaz into your life to help things move or to create a glamorous mist around them.

You'll need your journal, a timer and something comfortable to sit on. I use a meditation cushion, but a sofa or chair is fine.

- ❖ In your journal, draw or write Isaz four times.
- ❖ Then make yourself comfortable – sitting cross-legged helps – and set your timer for three minutes.
- ❖ Make fists with both hands and bring them to the centre of your chest, knuckles touching each other. Point your thumbs upwards towards your head.

- ✦ Hold this position and close your eyes. Take long, deep breaths.

- ✦ When the alarm goes off, journal what came up.

- ✦ You can do this over and over for about an hour, with a five-minute break in the middle if that feels good. Any longer than that and the energy will get too big to control and insert itself into your life in unexpected or unpleasant ways.

Affirmation

'I am true to myself.'

JERA

Yer-Ra

Sound

The 'yh' in 'Yule', 'yellow' or 'yowzer'.

Inspiration

Working towards goals.

Gift

Success/completion.

Challenge

Lost momentum.

Old rune poem

> *Ger byÞ gumena hiht, ðonne God læteþ,*
>
> *halig heofones cyning,*
>
> *hrusan syllan beorhte bleda beornum ond ðearfum*

> *The year is a joy for the men when the god,*
> *godly king of the skies,*
> *makes earth supply brightly the noble and the*
> *poor.*

Jera is the end of summer, the end of growth, the end of warmth. In Viking times, and even now, when the year begins to turn towards autumn/fall, we harvest our crops. Jera energy is that of the harvest, of completion and success. Back in the day, the success of the summer was vital in ensuring the people had all they needed to survive the winter.

So, Jera is reaping the rewards of our hard work over the course of time. The rewards are hard-earned, not instant. Seeds don't become fruit overnight.

Also, we have to put the effort in. Jera will give us rewards, but not if we just sit back and simply expect them to show up.

Jera here and now

In the now, Jera is the payday at the end of the month, the annual leave that we desperately need. It's the deadline for the essay, or the cut-off point for a race. It's the sense of completion when the programme finishes, or the tomatoes ripen and we can eat them.

When we're working on a project, Jera is the final push required to finish it. Then it is that feeling of a job well done.

It's an interesting phenomenon that in our modern world we want to push things through to fruition. This push often results in things that aren't as complete as they could be, like force-growing vegetables in poly-tunnels on a massive scale. In one way this is great, as it feeds lots of people; the flip side is that when we push too hard to finish something early, it may not be completed in the most beneficial way. In the case of fast-grown tomatoes, the result is fewer nutrients, less flavour and a weaker plant. Jera is things coming to fruition, completion and manifestation in the fullness of time. If we put in the required time and energy, we *will* get our reward.

Building a relationship with Jera

Jera is patient, relaxed and inevitable. To work with Jera, start something, work on it, finish it, get the reward. That is the basic form of Jera.

Some ways to use Jera energy:

❖ Place the rune in your veg patch or garden to encourage full growth, maybe drawing it on a lollipop stick or etching into plant pots.

❖ You could also use Jera on your harvesting tools, to encourage the harvest.

❖ Jera on a bank statement or stock certificate will encourage growth and eventual harvest. Remember, if you don't specify an end date, then maturity will take place in its own time, and you'll have to guess when that is. Bitcoin, for example, back in the early 2000s was a novelty worth cents, and is now worth much more. This maturing is the energy of Jera.

When Jera shows up

❖ What needs more energy in order to be completed?

❖ Where is there a harvest you have not claimed?

❖ Where are there loose ends you need to tie up?

❖ What needs more time?

❖ What are you rushing?

Jera in a reading brings the idea of completion or harvest to the question. Things may be ready for you to act on or ready for you to complete so you can move on to the next thing. 'Ready' is a good word with Jera.

Jera could also mean that you've got to give an idea time to mature, rather than rush it.

Context matters. With 'Should I ask her to marry me after a second date?', the Jera response may be: 'Let things mature first,' whereas with 'It's been 10 years –

should I ask her to marry me?', the Jera response could be: 'She's ready now.'

If Jera shows up in the wild, take a look at your personal world and see what needs to mature or what has matured enough. A little introspection is required here. Is the rune being attracted to the energy of a project or a personal thing?

Jera meditation

For this meditation, grab your timer and journal and find somewhere comfortable to sit. I do this on a yoga mat, sitting on a cushion.

❖ Either draw or write Jera three times in your journal.

❖ Set your timer for three minutes.

❖ Sit up straight and bring your hands level with your heart, palms facing down.

❖ Bring your thumbs together, then put both of them into the palm of your left hand – left thumb bent, right straight. This makes the fingers of both hands point straight out, and the hands come in front of each other, with the right outermost, like stegosaurus spines.

❖ Look at the tip of your nose and breathe easily. Inhale and say to yourself, 'Jera.' Then exhale and say, 'Jera.'

❖ You are going to multitask now. Keeping up the internal 'Jera' chant, on the inhale imagine bringing your belly button to your nose.

✦ Do this for three minutes, then journal what you feel.

This meditation brings the energy of Jera to your life-force, your *Ond*, which resides in your tummy, to help you complete the tasks or projects you've got on your to-do list today.

Affirmation

'All things come to fruition at the correct time.'

EIHWAZ

Yeehu-Waz

Sound

The 'yuh' sound in 'yew' or 'yoghurt' and the sound of the word 'why'.

Inspiration

Stored potential.

Gift

Harnessing potent energy.

Challenge

Hoarding useless energy.

Old rune poem

> *Eoh byþ utan unsmeþe treow,*
>
> *heard hrusan fæst, hyrde fyres,*
>
> *wyrtrumun underwreþyd, wyn on eþle.*

> *Yew is a tree, rough on the outside,*
> *Hard and fast in the earth, a shepherd of the fire,*
> *His roots under the pillar, a joy on the native land.*

Eihwaz is the yew tree, a tree that is traditionally placed away from grazing animals and in sacred spaces. There are several reasons for this. If grazing animals eat the fruits of the tree, they die, and if you sit under the yew tree in high summer, the aroma it emits is psychoactive. The ancient peoples of the world used to spend a pleasant afternoon this way. Especially the priestesses and priests of pre-Abrahamic religions.

Other properties of the yew that are of interest here are that it is slow-burning, and the ancients used to carry smouldering embers from place to place in yew carriers. This quality of slow-burning resilience and longevity is also one aspect of the rune Eihwaz.

The other is its sheer power. Back in the days before gunpowder, the only power available was muscle power, and the bow was the best way to launch a projectile. A yew bow was able to store tremendous amounts of potential energy, and indeed propel an arrow through plate armour. Even in the age of gunpowder, one British general wished for longbowmen rather than musketeers, as they could fire faster and further. These qualities of skill and stored potential are also an aspect of Eihwaz.

Eihwaz here and now

Eihwaz inspires us to look to what we already have, know and have experienced to fuel envisioned action.

The flip side of this is to look to how we are wasting our time/energy or where we're simply not using our creativity and energy effectively, because Eihwaz can encourage us to store it for a time when it's 'useful'.

Energy cannot be stored infinitely; it does need to be used up. If you have a tendency to inaction, know that your energy will potentially be wasted. Stored energy can fade. Batteries will slowly lose their electrical charge. When we store energy, it's the same – it gets leached away by the cosmos. But as long as the embers are smouldering, there's the potential for them to be sparked into flame.

This is where the envisioned action comes in – don't push too hard in January, for example, if you're planning an event in June. Instead store that energy, feed it daily until it's actually useful. Like a battery, charge it up slowly but surely until it's ready to be used.

Building a relationship with Eihwaz

✦ Eihwaz is a great rune to put on items that you want to hold energy – sacred tools, wands, drums, crystal bags, etc.

✦ Putting it on an altar to store energy for a later ritual is a good use.

✦ Putting it on your lighter will help the flame keep going.

✦ Putting it next to your bed will help you dream dreams of power.

✦ Putting it on something that stores energy, like a battery pack or your phone, will help it hold more, but make sure the intent is for longer battery power, for example, as heat isn't good in a phone!

✦ When at an event or with a person you're vibing with, or whose energy you really like, maybe at a gig, or when seeing your favourite speaker or an inspiring friend, take a bottle of water and whisper to it, 'Please hold the energy of this experience.' Write the Eihwaz rune on the bottle and enjoy your day. The water will hold the energetic resonance around you. Drink the water in front of your altar to bring that energy into your physical form. As you drink it, you'll activate that energy within you.

I've got water from a glacier in Norway, ice from Iceland, precious water from the desert and water from good times with friends. Each stores the energy of that time and place and I either use a few drops in magical projects, put a few drops in the bath or add a few drops to drinking water to reactivate the energy of those adventures.

The challenge of Eihwaz is that it can store *all* the energy around you, which is great if you are a high-vibing, juice-drinking, vegan CrossFitter who looks after old people and injured birds 24/7. But most of us *aren't*. We have other influences that can create and attract energy that's not so useful. Think supermarket trips, driving in snarly traffic, constant information feeds, viruses. Eihwaz likes to store the energy we access most, as it recognizes that we are likely to use it most. Smart, eh? Except if our energy is mostly spent fretting, worrying and feeling anxious, that is the energy that will be stored. It's the same as training a puppy. If the pup is used to being shouted at, it will only respond to being shouted at; if it is instructed calmly and firmly, then that's what it will respond to.

If drama is your thing, Eihwaz will store it. If hugging puppies is your thing, Eihwaz will store it. If you spend time dancing, moving, manifesting, reading books and watching material that nourishes you, Eihwaz will store it. Get the idea?

If you simply let energy come, be prepared to receive a mixed bag. If you'd like Eihwaz to support you in storing more of the energies that you want easy access to more often, then your daily work is to consciously choose the thoughts, emotions and actions whose energy you want Eihwaz to store.

Another way to build a relationship with Eihwaz is to connect to the yew tree. Connecting with trees has been done for millennia, and now science has caught up and there are lots of studies that suggest what we've known all along: being in woods and forests helps us feel more relaxed.

Let me share three different ways to connect to the yew tree, ranging from easy to hard.

❖ This one you can do from your bed or sofa. Write or draw Eihwaz in your journal. Then find some yew wood, hold it in your non-dominant hand and meditate on what Eihwaz and/or the yew tree would like you to know. Meditating is very indicative of Eihwaz, as it's a way to collect and store your own inner resources, so pay attention to what comes through. Hold the wood as you slowly breathe with the intent of connecting to Eihwaz.

❖ Go out and find a yew tree. In Europe they tend to be in old churchyards. Once you've found one, stop, take a breath and ask the tree spirit if you can approach. A 'yes' will be shown by a change in the environment – a bird suddenly taking flight, a twig falling or a change in the wind. You will know it when it happens. Then go and hug the tree. Yews can be quite big, as they live for hundreds of years, so you may not be able to get your arms all the way around it. That doesn't matter. Just give yourself a few minutes to hug, feel the vibrational force, thank the tree, then journal what came through.

✦ This one needs hot weather. Go out and find a yew tree, taking some water with you, as you'll be spending a good couple of hours with it. Get permission to approach, then sit down under the tree. Slow your breath and breathe deeply. Write/ draw the Eihwaz rune in your journal and then focus on your breath. When you start to relax, you can lie down or continue sitting, whichever is comfortable. When you are ready, you can journal what is coming to you from Eihwaz and the yew.

As a point, don't eat any of the yew berries or needles. They are toxic.

When Eihwaz shows up

✦ Where is energy needed?

✦ Where is energy being held onto needlessly?

✦ What new energy can be held?

✦ Where is there the potential to release energy in a meaningful way?

In a reading, Eihwaz is the connection to the energy of your choosing, or the question you're asking. Yet again, context matters here. What can be released? What can be retained and carried? See where this duality can be harnessed by the other runes in the reading.

Because of the yew's poisonous and hallucinatory nature, Eihwaz can be seen as a rune of death, of connection to other worlds. In a reading, it can mean that there is the possibility of connection to the other side.

If Eihwaz shows up when you are out and about, be present to the energies that you are harbouring. What needs to be there? What can be released? Remember you can turn energy into action.

Eihwaz meditation

Choosing what energy to pick up and what to discard is a practice in self-discipline. This meditation helps you sift through the energies that you have encountered during the day.

✦   As you lie in bed, having done all the pre-sleep things you do, run through the things of the day that are still with you – you know, the thoughts that you dwell on and that take up valuable head space.

✦   Then, look at what you can learn from them, be it act differently, hold your temper for a fraction longer, pay a tiny bit more attention, etc.

❖ Then dismiss the event. Magically, this closes the circle of the event in your own personal energy field.

❖ This way you can choose to store the positive learning energy from the day's events, and not be stuck with 'if only' energy. 'If only' energy is quite frankly rubbish.

This is an everyday practice, and it becomes easier the more you do it.

Affirmation

'I am master/mistress of my own energy.'

PEROTH

Per-oth

Sound
The 'puh' in 'penny', 'piece' and 'pat'.

Inspiration
The joy of companionship.

Gift
Good fortune.

Challenge
Less than good fortune.

Old rune text

> *Peorð byþ symble plega and hlehter*
>
> *wlancum, ðar wigan sittaþ on beorsele bliþe*
> *ætsomne.*

> *Peroth is the feast day, the games and casting by lots,*
>
> *for the proud fighters sitting in the mead hall, happy together.*

The runic energy of Peroth brings the essence of what the proud fighters felt in the Viking hall together, celebrating, feasting and having fun, often after fighting for their lives. This rune resonates with a relatively large sphere of human life:

* *Sex:* This is pretty obvious, as the rune looks like a pair of wide-open legs. Sex for fun was frowned upon by the ancient Nordic people. But sex for babies was a sacred act. We can tell this from the number of statues of gods with a giant phallus and goddesses with fertility symbols, like grain, distaffs or cats. This implies the magical power of sex in the Nordic cultural identity. Indeed, the monks who went to document the rituals in Uppsala, Sweden, on a fertility holy day refused to document them, as they were too indecent.

* *Chance:* Games of chance, from cards to dice, have always been played where people have gathered together, and the ancient Nordic people were no different. Being supremely proficient bone and wood workers, the ancient peoples of the north created intricate dice of many different shapes and sizes.

❖ *Fate:* This is a modern interpretation of the rune, trying to fit the idea of chance with the *Wyrd*. As covered elsewhere, though, chance is not *Wyrd*. This rune is not a *Wyrd* rune, it's a rune of chance and sex. The *Wyrd* is present in all of the runes.

Meaning Making

Peroth is one of my favourite runes, because its meaning is so nebulous. This rune sums up in a few lines what happens when one culture appropriates another culture's beliefs and patterns without understanding them or, worse, while deliberately misinterpreting them.

Peroth speaks of what people do when feasting. Especially proud fighters. Now, fighters tended to be young men at the time, and what do young men do when they want to unwind after doing a stressful thing like fighting? I'm talking about sex. But the people who translated the oral history of the Nordic people were celibate monks living sheltered lives in monasteries. So they called it being 'happy together'.

This is a perfect example of cultural bias. However, one of the best things about the runes, through an esoteric lens, is that your perceived meaning is as valid as mine, or that of someone who has done a PhD on them. The phonetics are pretty set, but the esoteric meaning is very much up for personal interpretation.

Peroth here and now

In the here and now, Peroth is luck, physical love and fate. Individually or in any combination. But it mainly brings luck. The ancient Nordic people had different words for luck. Peroth resonates with this one: *Hamingja*, the luck you have to earn. As hinted at in the poem, *Hamingja* is not made in isolation; it needs the people around you to add to it. Having fun with your friends builds your *Hamingja*, and this in turn helps good things happen to you. I'm sure you've found that when you're feeling low and isolated, good things are hard to come by, but when you're feeling good and connected, good things are easier to come by. This is Peroth in action: the rune is attracted to the good-vibe energy of people being in community and living life.

Building a relationship with Peroth

❖ *Go out:* The first and foremost way of building a powerful relationship with Peroth is to go to a place where this energy resides. Introverts, I know this is not your happy place, but I'm sorry to say you're going to have to interact with people to get the magic of this rune. Still, don't worry. It's being around people you love and respect and who love and respect you that will bring the energy of Peroth to you. Incidentally, remember, please, that love and respect aren't granted, they are earned.

❖ *Socialize:* The more good-quality interaction with other people you experience, in a way that nourishes you and fills you up, the more Peroth and *Hamingja* energy will come to you. Shared interests, hanging out with people for fun, or working in an environment that is mutually beneficial, like a good team, will all build this energy. Remember, hanging around people who don't value you, or whom you yourself don't value, won't attract this good fortune. In fact, it will repel it.

❖ *Interact:* Peroth is an energy of shared experience and human interaction, but dogs count too, as do horses, cats... no, actually, not so much. Interacting with people is the grade A. It's by building community energy by bouncing off other people that our energy fields change and we attract good fortune. This is Peroth.

When Peroth shows up

Peroth in the wild is a sign of changing fortunes. So, check whether you are relying too heavily on your luck to move you forward, and see where you can build it up or reduce that over-reliance. Remember, the Norns are capricious, and if they see you resting on your laurels, they will knock your feet out from under you.

In a reading, Peroth also suggests a change in fortune – communal fortune usually. Be aware in the context of the reading where the client is lacking in fortune or luck, or where there is an overabundance of this energy.

When talking about romance in a reading, Peroth suggests sexual attraction, lust and sex. Again, context is important. This is where you should use your skills as an oracle to delve into the situation behind the client's question.

Peroth meditation

This is probably the most Viking-like meditation in this book. So, go get a drink/get a meal/raid a monastery/lay siege to Paris, etc., safely, with friends you trust.

Seriously, go – go outside, go hang out with people, go to a gig, a bar or pub, sing songs, go to a communal ritual honouring the season, dance with friends.

If you're an introvert, start small by building your trust with one or two people. Know where your boundaries are and push them slightly every day. Allow yourself to trust others and make friends.

Affirmation

> *'I am able to choose the fortune
> that favours me.'*

ALGIZ

Al-Geez

Sound
The 'ex' in 'X-ray', 'expect', 'exact' or 'eggs'.

Inspiration
The creative use of technology or nature.

Gift
Protection from malevolent energies.

Challenge
Over-reliance on the external for protection.

Old rune poem
> *Eolh-secg eard hæfþ oftust on fenne*
> *wexeð on wature, wundaþ grimme,*
> *blode breneð beorna gehwylcne*
> *ðe him ænigne onfeng gedeþ.*

The elk-sedge often dwells in fens,
grows in water, grimly wounds
and burns with boils the blood
of the hero who seizes it.

In the deep recesses of history, people lived in places where they could easily get clean water and good food. Some lived in the rolling hills of Wessex, others in the frozen fjords of Norway, others in the Frisian marshes. Common to all these places are deer, and in the north, elk, whose proud horns ward off enemies. The people who lived in the north saw what the elk did and copied them, using thorns and barriers of wood to protect themselves. In Wessex they dug forts, in the fens they built their homes on stilts, in Norway they made turf and wood fences and homes. Algiz is about using what nature has given us and our own inventiveness to build defences to keep ourselves safe from predators, be they human or animal.

There is another aspect of this rune, too. Algiz is not just defensive and adaptive, it is also mystical. It is the swan. The swan's mighty wings can break a bone, while its smooth elegance has been described as a gift from the divine. The grace of the swan and the power of its wings reach up to the skies like the elk's horns.

Algiz here and now

Here and now, Algiz is a rune of protection, and is often used in amulets and rituals for that singular purpose.

There is more to it than that, though. Algiz is attracted to the energy of adaptation, technology and innovation. It's not enough to put a fence up. We ensure our continued safety by using our imagination and creativity to make our defences consistently strong. So, Algiz marries the natural world with the innovation of the human mind to bring creativity into technology. It is this ability to adapt and overcome that raises us up from the mud. Algiz is the connection to divine inspiration, its shape not just that of antlers or swan's wings, but of a chalice catching the drops of inspiration from the gods.

Building a relationship with Algiz

❖ Putting Algiz on your house or garden walls is a great way to bring in its protective energy. My garden fence has it on each panel, as do my house walls – it's etched in charcoal and covered by a coat of paint.

❖ It's also about setting good personal boundaries – not agreeing to pick someone up from an airport at 3 a.m. when you really don't want to. Establishing strong boundaries is part of building your energy or personal *Ond*. But we are designed to be in community, and not being fluid with how you interact with people will deplete your energy and leave you a husk.

✦ This energetic exchange also extends to the divine. With good boundaries, and with practice, you can choose how you connect to the cosmos. This is especially useful if you have interesting dreams or if spirits or the dead come and bother you when you are trying to sleep. Or if you want them to.

✦ If you want to draw down inspiration from the gods, carve Algiz on a piece of fruit wood, like the branch of a fruit tree or the stem of an apple or pear, and put it under your pillow before you sleep. It will also keep away bad dreams.

✦ Algiz helps with innovation, and inventiveness as well. It's on the notebook that I use to scribble ideas in, helping me keep them safe and get as much inspiration as possible!

When Algiz shows up

✦ Where are your boundaries?

✦ What barriers do you have in place that are stopping you from doing what you want to do?

✦ How is your creative use of tech or nature manifesting?

✦ Where are you being too defensive?

✦ Where are you not being defensive enough?

In the wild, Algiz suggests that there might be boundary issues going on for you. These could be emotional, physical, professional or personal.

If you see Algiz at an event or gathering, look to where your energetic walls are. This is an important realization, as when there are lots of people together for an event, there is a lot of combined energy. While this is great, remember that there's always the chance of energetic overspill, and you definitely don't want to pick up someone's rubbish energy.

In a reading, Algiz often indicates defence or protection. Look there first, then move your gaze to technology, adaptation and connection to the divine. This energy could mean that physical boundaries are being crossed – maybe a garden fence is broken or the front door lock isn't as secure as it could be. Start with the mundane and work up from there. Context will help. If the client is asking about romance, Algiz could signify their barriers are too strong to let anyone in. If they are asking about work, perhaps their barriers are too slack and they are getting dumped on.

Algiz meditation

This is a boundary-setting meditation. You will need your journal and a timer, pen and comfy thing to sit on.

✦ Start by sitting on the floor, with your right leg straight and flat on the floor, and your left leg bent with your knee straight up, toes pointing forwards.

✦ Put the sole of your left foot on the side of your right foot, with the ball of your left foot just lower than the rise of your right ankle.

✦ Make your left hand into a fist and put it knuckles down on the ground by your left hip.

✦ Bring your right elbow to your right knee, so you are twisted slightly.

✦ Then bring your right hand to your right ear. Make your right hand a cup and put it over your right ear, to bring the energy back into your body.

✦ Got it? Unwind yourself and get your journal.

✦ Next, write the Algiz rune three times in your journal, along with the boundary you want to set. For example, 'I want to be able to say "no" to my boss when she makes unreasonable requests.'

✦ Set your timer for three minutes, resume your position and close your eyes.

✦ Softly chant, 'Al-Geez,' softly to yourself.

✤ Imagine a bubble of force around you, a boundary coming from your heart space that is your boundary for this energy. You can infuse your energy construct with the Algiz rune as well.

✤ When you've done this for three minutes, change sides for three more minutes on the other side. You want an even bubble, right?

✤ Then journal your thoughts.

Affirmation

'I set and maintain my own boundaries.'

SOWOLIO

Sow-ol-io

Sound
The 'esss' in 'sun', 'sea' and… 'sauna'.

Inspiration
Guidance.

Gift
Seeing the path.

Challenge
Casting too big a shadow.

Old rune text

Sigel semannum symble biþ on hihte, ðonne hi hine feriaþ ofer fisces beþ, oþ hi brimhengest bringeþ to lande.

The sun is ever a joy in the hopes of seafarers when they journey away over the fishes' bath, until the courses of the deep bring them to land.

Fifteen hundred years ago we didn't have compasses, clocks or any way to navigate at sea. If we were without stars or landmarks, we had to use the sun. As the sun rises in the east and sets in the west, solar navigation means that we know where east and west are, and so where north and south are. This means that we can navigate relatively safely.

In a similar way, the sun is our guiding light in life. In the frozen north, its warmth meant that life could return to the land each year.

Sowolio has the energies of knowing where to go and the life that comes from the sun.

It's important to remember that the length of the winter nights in Scandinavia, especially as you go further north, makes the return of the sun even more welcome. After the darkness of winter, the snow melts and the crops grow. That's a powerful transformation.

Sowolio here and now

So, Sowolio is life-giving energy. It is receiving guidance and finding our way in uncharted waters. We're great at surviving the unknown, we've evolved to be able to handle that, and what makes it possible is the ability to know where we are.

When we know where we are, and where we've come from, we can work out where we're going. This is the power of Sowolio – navigation, either when physically travelling or when working out how our life is going to pan out.

Sowolio is the guiding star that shows us where our decisions, our behaviour and our habits are taking us. This personal compass allows us to adjust our heading and change our destination.

When called upon, Sowolio can shine light on the path ahead, so we can see our destination and perhaps avoid some of the pitfalls along the way. If we are lost energetically or emotionally, its energy can help bring us back to where we want to be.

Building a relationship with Sowolio

Sowolio is great for looking for the direction to take in life as well as on a journey.

- ❖ Put it on your outdoors stuff, like your rucksack, boots, compass and map case.

- ❖ Put a Sowolio sticker on your GPS and/or on the dashboard of your car. However you choose to navigate the world, navigation can be energetically improved with Sowolio.

✦ Sowolio is a great tool for navigating cosmic pathways too. Wearing it on a pendant or having it by your bed will bring direction and guidance to meditative and astral travel practices.

When Sowolio shows up

✦ What is your goal?

✦ Why are you on this path?

✦ Where is guidance needed?

In the wild, Sowolio means that there is a path for you to take, and you can take it or not. That is your choice.

A wild Sowolio will point in the direction of or to the energy that is beckoning you. Is it on a path? Is it on a sign? Is it on the shirt or tee of a super-attractive person? See this as a 'this will be an interesting and powerful experience if you take the next step' kind of vibe.

In a reading, Sowolio will point to the direction to take. Look at the context, the client's needs and their question, as well as any runes that may be close to this one. You can definitely draw another rune to add more context here.

Sowolio meditation

For this meditation you will need your journal, somewhere comfortable to sit and some flash cards.

❖ Draw or write Sowolio three times in your journal.

❖ Then draw or write it on one of the flash cards. Spend a few minutes putting the runic energy of direction-seeking into the card. You can do this with thought and mental constructs, or write on the card if this works better for you.

❖ Then fold the card into the shape of an aeroplane, and, in daylight, so the sun is shining (somewhere), launch the plane into the air. Where it lands will indicate the direction you're being guided to take. So, you're being guided towards nature, if it lands in a potted plant, or towards technology, if it lands near a router. Use your intuition to see where the rune is guiding you.

❖ Then journal with it.

Affirmation

'I have direction and I know where I'm going.'

TIWAZ

Tee-Waz or Tay-Waz

Sound

The hard 'tuh' in 'twitch', 'trampoline' or 'tickle'.

Inspiration

Morally correct action.

Gift

The courage to act according to your values.

Challenge

Rigid adhesion to doctrine.

Old rune text

Tir biþ tacna sum, healdeð trywa wel wiþ æþelingas; a biþ on færylde ofer nihta genipu, næfre swiceþ.

> *Tir is one of the signs; it keeps its promise with the noble, and it is there during the journey above the dark of the night; it never deceives.*

Ethics and values played a strong part in ancient Nordic culture, as people had to depend on one another for survival on the seas and during the cold winters. The land can be harsh in Norway, Iceland and other northern areas. To survive, you need to be able to trust your neighbours and they need to be able to trust you.

Back in the day, we had no list of criminals that the authorities would look for, or ways of doing background checks, and quite frankly, everyone was heavily armed. So we had to trust that people had a code of ethics that they stood by.

Tiwaz is the rune of that trust and honour. Not the honour we read about in fantasy literature, but the honour of doing the right thing no matter what. Of following our code of ethics as we live our life.

Tiw, Tir or Tyr is the god of this concept. He sacrificed his right arm to make sure that the world was safe from destruction (the story can be found in the Resources at the back of the book).

Tiwaz here and now

Today, ethics are enshrined in law, and communal ethics are defined by law-makers. This works, for the most part, because our populations have grown and we are unable to trust that complete strangers have the same values as we do, and communal laws fill that gap.

There is a link between Tiwaz and justice, but that is a 19th-century adaptation. Tiwaz isn't laws, it isn't the modern concept of justice, it's a personal code of ethics. We all know someone who gets the job done, makes sure the people around them are safe and operates according to their code of ethics, even though they may not operate within the law. Doing what is right in the face of opposition is the Rule of Tiwaz – protesting the building of oil pipelines on stolen land, standing up to bullies and doing what is right by your group, tribe or clan.

I'm not talking nation states here, I'm talking groups of up to 150-ish, the community size we evolved into. The group we belong to, through our own choice, will have its own set of moral codes and rules. Tiwaz is the upholding of those rules, not through coercion, but through doing the right thing.

Building a relationship with Tiwaz

Building a relationship with Tiwaz is super hard or super easy. It depends on how you view the rules of the culture you live in.

If you are living in a world that challenges your values and beliefs, standing by them can be hard, but constantly betraying your own values can cause anxiety and depression.

Tiwaz is a powerful rune that will help you to act in line with your values when all around you are flailing. This is especially useful when there is a stress factor in society, as people often let their morals slip when they are afraid or faced with a threat. A good rule of thumb is: 'Don't behave in ways that you wouldn't like others to behave in.'

The key to working with Tiwaz is to be true to your values and beliefs, and to recognize that as you change, grow and learn, they may change too. However, changing your mind from one day to the next will make you someone who cannot be trusted. It is through consistently standing by your values and beliefs that you will build a good relationship with Tiwaz.

Right and wrong in ancient Scandinavia

Murder was illegal in Viking times, and the penalty for it very high. The definition was, however, different from now. Murder was ambushing someone or attacking them from behind. And then killing them. If you squared up to them in the street and killed them in a face-to-face fight, it was not murder, but killing. There was a penalty for killing, but it was less severe, as killing was seen as a thing that happened.

Be aware that others may not view the world in the same way you do. In your culture, for example, would killing and murder be the same?

. . . .

When Tiwaz shows up

❖ What do you value most highly?

❖ When do you find your honour being challenged?

❖ Where are your values or beliefs being challenged now?

❖ What stops you from acting on your beliefs?

In the wild, Tiwaz is pointing towards an act or behaviour that is likely to challenge your values. This literal arrow could be pointing towards the situation or the solution. Be aware of how it shows up and in what context.

In a reading, Tiwaz implies that there is an element of honour in the solution to the client's question. Are they currently not acting in accordance with their values and beliefs or are those values being challenged externally? Either way, sticking by their beliefs will be part of the solution.

Tiwaz meditation

Doing the right thing can be hard and it takes constant practice. Here is a daily meditation that will help.

As you lie in bed at the end of the day, bring to mind the things that you did during the day – and *only* during the day – that were *not* in accordance with your beliefs and values. Without passion or anger, see why you acted in that way. Ask yourself what caused this behaviour. Remember that unless they are holding a gun to your head, no one can make you do anything.

Find out why you felt you needed to act in ways that were not in accordance with your values. Look at where your needs were not being met, where you needed more support. Were you hungry? Thirsty? Did you feel afraid? Or under pressure? What could you have asked for to support yourself, so you did not have to act in that way?

What can you learn from the situation that means you will be less likely to act in that way again?

Learn, journal it, drop the situation and move on.

Affirmation

*'I always remain true to myself
and my values and beliefs.'*

BERKANAN

Ber-karn-an

Sound

The 'buh' in 'bee', 'birch' or 'bottom'.

Inspiration

Regrowth.

Gift

Recovery.

Challenge

Withdrawal from society.

Old rune poem

Beorc byþ bleda leas, bereþ efne swa ðeah
tanas butan tudder, biþ on telgum wlitig,
heah on helme hrysted fægere,
geloden leafum, lyfte getenge.

> *Birch has no shoots;*
> *it carries its rods without fruits;*
> *Radiant high twigs, high its crown*
> *with leaves fairly laden, reaches the sky.*

There are two aspects to Berkanan: the birch and the bear. They have similar energies but are subtly different.

The birch tree works to make the land more fertile, even when the soil has been badly burned by forest fire or has had a lot of pine trees growing on it, making it acidic. This 'pioneer tree' revitalizes the soil with the enzymes in its roots, allowing the oak, ash, alder and the rest of the forest to have fertile ground in which to regrow.

So, Berkanan-birch is the act of renewal and regeneration.

The other aspect of Berkanan, the bear, *bjønan*, is related to this. Bears were both feared and respected in the wilderness of the frozen north, from the brown bears of the south to the white bears of the islands of the far north. Unfortunately, the native European ones were hunted almost to extinction across most of the continent 1,000 years ago.

Bears have the ability to withstand great hardships and to take themselves away to their den to rest, heal and give birth in a safe environment. This subterranean healing is a powerful resonance of Berkanan.

Berkanan-bear is the cave time before the regeneration, the resilience before the renewal.

Berkanan here and now

In the here and now, Berkanan is the energy that turns a toxic environment into a fertile one. This is great in toxic offices and work environments. Please remember birch takes 20 years to grow, so there won't be quick results, but Berkanan is the energy of lots of little changes bringing about healing over time.

In a toxic office, Berkanan is the energy of keeping your head down to make sure that you have the resilience you need before moving on to the next thing. It's hibernating through the toxicity.

Both Berkanan aspects require endurance and staying power while subtly doing the work to heal. Berkanan is this energy of resilience, renewal and regeneration.

Building a relationship with Berkanan

Berkanan is best inscribed or marked on things that you have with you all the time, like house keys or a phone case. This way, its healing resonance is with you constantly.

❖ If you are struggling with rest and recovery, put the Berkanan rune on your bed frame or on the bottom of the sofa. It will bring the energy of the bear's cave to your comfy places to help you heal, recover and revive.

✦ If you're someone who loves resting and recovering a little too much, it might be worth having the symbol on a sticker or piece of wood that you can put in the space and take out of the space when you need to get up and do some work, for example.

✦ Place Berkanan anywhere you experience stress or stickiness, as its energy has the capacity to transmute it into something more useful, like action or healing. You get to choose. Just make your intention clear.

✦ Place the rune on your water bottle. It will activate the energy of rejuvenation and healing in the water, so that when you drink it, it will activate that energy within you too.

When Berkanan shows up

Berkanan in the wild marks a period of regeneration and recovery. Look to situations where you can make little changes to help turn the toxic fertile – tiny improvements that will eventually make the world a better place.

A wild Berkanan could also be a clue to start getting ready to metaphorically hibernate through a storm that is coming.

In a reading, Berkanan signifies that small changes need to happen to resolve the question. The toxic needs to be alchemized to get the desired outcome. It could also mean that unpleasantness needs to be weathered or hidden from until it has passed, to allow new growth.

Berkanan meditation

Berkanan is an earth rune, as all the birch and bear energy is subterranean, so an earth ritual is the best way to connect to its energy. Here are two examples:

You can do the first ritual from your bed or sofa:

❖ Get some birch wood, hold it in your hand and meditate on Berkanan and the birch tree.

❖ Hold the wood in your non-dominant hand while you draw or write the rune in your journal.

❖ Breathe slowly and let it speak through you.

For the second ritual, you'll need to go outside:

❖ Go and find a birch tree. In Europe they tend to be in older woodlands and have small oval or elliptical leaves and a slender, silvery trunk. They are different the world over, so the internet will be your friend.

❖ Once you've found your birch tree, stop, take a breath, and ask if you can approach. A 'yes' will be shown by a change in the environment – a bird suddenly taking flight, a twig falling or a change in the wind. You will know it when it happens.

❖ When you have it, go and hug the tree. Birches can be just the right size to hug, so you may be able to get your arms right round.

- ❖ Give yourself a few minutes to feel the energy of the tree and all it knows.

- ❖ When you're ready, thank it for sharing its energy with you.

- ❖ Journal the experience.

Affirmation

> *'I am resilient. I am not my environment.'*

EHWAZ

Eh-Waz

Sound

The 'eh' in 'egg', 'head' and 'edible'.

Inspiration

A trusted friend.

Gift

True trust and companionship.

Challenge

Over-dependence on others.

Old rune poem

Eh byþ for eorlum æþelinga wyn,

hors hofum wlanc, ðær him hæleþ ymb[e] welege
on wicgum wrixlaþ

spræce and biþ unstyllum æfre frofur.

> *Steed is for the prince's and the noble's joy;*
>
> *the warhorse arrogant in the hall where the wealthy heroes exchange talk.*
>
> *And it is ever refuge to the unstill ones.*

Back in the day, horses weren't ridden into battle like we see in the movies. There were no mounted cavalry charges. And horses then were much smaller, much closer in size to Icelandic ponies.

The Icelandic horse is the most trusted servant.

OLD ICELANDIC PROVERB

This rune looks like two horses' heads meeting together, nose to nose, and in Proto-Indo-European, the language of our ancient ancestors, *Ehwaz* means 'the swift one'. The resonance of Ehwaz is the swiftness and power of the horse and the trust in the other being – the divine connection to the other.

The ability to be 'unstill', as the poem says, is a powerful one – the power to travel at speed is game-changing. The Romans knew this; their legions used native cavalry to control large areas that men on foot could not manage. The ability to push boundaries political, martial, personal and spiritual is also one of the powers of the Ehwaz runic energy.

Being able to move faster than others means you have more freedom and more opportunities. You can also see further on a horse. Even a pony puts your eyeline above those of the peasants who are walking beside you. This is why horses were the province of the elite back in the day, especially in Norway and Iceland. The resources needed to keep an animal that was not milked or used to work a farm were substantial. Being able to widen your perspective by travelling, and travelling faster than people could walk, also brought a powerful opportunity for self-development and reputation-building.

Ehwaz is the rune of this privilege of travel and the abilities to see past and push past the boundaries between worlds.

Horses are part of the *Völva*'s magic too, representing their ability to travel between the worlds or planes of existence, or along the *Wyrd*. The association between powerful women and horses in Viking times has been shown by graves that have been excavated. In Birka, Sweden, for example, a woman was buried with rich jewellery, a sword, distaff and two horses. This could well have been the grave of a powerful *Völva*, using the magic of Ehwaz to travel between the worlds on her spiritual journeys.

Ehwaz here and now

These days, Ehwaz is an energy that is used often and almost thoughtlessly. Jumping on a plane to another coast, continent, culture or country is a daily occurrence. We no longer value long-distance travel in the same way as in ancient times, when people rarely travelled more than 30 miles from home.

In those days, travelling from one side of Europe to the other took months of hazardous journeying, and this is where the magic of this rune lies. If the experience of travelling doesn't push your boundaries, then your boundaries stay static. Ehwaz is the experience of pushing your boundaries, allowing them to expand. This doesn't need to involve backpacking around Asia for six months; the energy can be seen in a toddler moving from clinging to their mother's leg to walking solo to the kitchen door. Every time you push to see more, feel more, experience more, you are working with Ehwaz.

Ehwaz is also the journey to the spirit realm, using drumbeats, psychedelia and/or other means of travel. When we use our innate human ability to travel to another realm or to 'horse' into the body of another creature, we are using the magic of Ehwaz. Astral projection, spirit journeys and spiritual healing all benefit from the energy of Ehwaz.

Whatever the context, Ehwaz is the adventure of being able to move fast to change our perspective.

Building a relationship with Ehwaz

Essentially, this involves expanding your world-view. There are many ways of doing it, including:

❖ Sitting on the top of a double-decker bus or going to the top floor of a building or tourist attraction.

❖ Putting Ehwaz on your passport case, luggage or travel bags to help you find the energy and experiences that you need when adventuring.

❖ Assuming you don't already have a horse, finding someone who will let you ride one, either a friend or a professional stable. This is a great way to get your horse energy on. When you are horsing about, feel the power of the animal and appreciate the extra view you get and the feeling of connection you develop as you move with the animal.

❖ Putting Ehwaz on wristbands or your clothes to bring that energy to you.

❖ Consciously pushing your boundaries – new food, new people, new places... This is a powerful way of expanding your world.

❖ Going on an adventure in your car, on your bike or even on a horse.

When Ehwaz shows up

In the wild, Ehwaz indicates energy is flowing to you that could broaden your horizons and send you on an adventure.

In a reading, Ehwaz implies that there is teamwork required and/or movement away from the current situation. Perhaps a change of perspective is what is needed? Or the stretching of boundaries? I've said it a lot, but context matters.

Ehwaz meditation

There are two parts to this meditation. You can do either or both. Or neither.

❖ Get yourself a bowl. I use a Pyrex one, as it's easy to clean.

❖ Fill it half full of water, then add black ink until you have a bowl of black water. Avoid spilling it – it makes a huge mess.

❖ Draw or write Ehwaz in your journal three times.

❖ Stare into the bowl with the intent of expanding your boundaries. Of journeying.

❖ Give yourself a few minutes. Let your focus slip and change as you gaze into the inky blackness.

❖ When you have finished, journal what came up for you.

Part 2

For the next part you'll need some stuff: a comfy nest, like a yoga mat and blanket, a way of playing an MP3, some mugwort or other means of space-clearing and your journal.

❖ In your journal, write out three times what you want to journey to see. Start small and then work up, for example from: 'Where did

I leave my keys?' to: 'How do I get promoted?'

✦ Draw or write Ehwaz three times in your journal and on the back of each hand. You could use make-up. I use a marker pen, but it's a pain to get off.

✦ Energetically cleanse the space around you. I use mugwort smoke sticks (they have a strong smell).

✦ Get clear in your mind what you are journeying for and make yourself a nest that is comfy to lie in. I use a yoga mat, sheepskins, a blanket, a bolster under my knees, an eye pillow and a pillow under my head.

✦ Read your intention in your journal again.

✦ In the Resources section at the back of the book, there is a link that will give you a free drum track. Put that track on your device.

✦ Settle down in your nest, and when you are ready, set the drum track going.

✦ Close your eyes and slow your breath. Allow your mind to follow the drumbeat and start your journey. Remember you are in charge of what happens when you travel. If you don't like it, command that you come back to your body.

✦ When the journey is over, the beat will change and call you back to your body. If your body has fallen asleep, that's fine, your spirit will still come back to it.

✦ When you come back to your body, journal what you came across on your journey.

Don't be disheartened if you can't do it first time. It's your first time.

Things that make it harder to travel can include pharmaceutical medication, stress, anxiety and small children or dogs jumping on you.

If this process isn't for you, just leave it and move on.

Affirmation

> *'I am allowed to expand my*
> *boundaries and perspective.'*

MANNAZ

Man-ahz

Sound
The 'ma' sound in 'man' and the 'muh' in 'mumma'.

Inspiration
The potential to achieve anything.

Gift
The power of being human.

Challenge
Being caught in the minutiae of life.

Old rune text

*Man byþ on myrgþe his magan leof: sceal þeah anra
gehwylc oðrum swican, forðum drihten wyle dome
sine þæt earme flæsc eorþan betæcan.*

> **A man is mirth to his beloved kin; he shall,
> though, each one deceive, when the Lord
> dooms his miserable flesh to be entrusted to
> the earth.**

A nice cheery poem here, and we can see the influence of the Christian monks who wrote it down. They wanted to make sure the Christian God was experienced as the most powerful force, and they did this by changing the language to that of their Bible, moving the power from the 'man' to the Lord.

With the runes, we are dealing with a language and an understanding of the world that are 1,500 years old. Just think how much language has evolved just in the last two decades. The runes hark back to a time when 'man' meant 'humanity', not just the masculine.

Humans have two main powers – physical and spiritual. This is an oversimplification, but, after all, this book is called *Runes Made Easy*. So, the powers are physical, as in everything that is or originates in the body, senses, mind, thoughts, muscles, etc., and spiritual, as in everything that extends past the body – energy, psychic abilities, etc.

The Nordic peoples knew these powers and weren't afraid to use them. In early medieval times, people lived hard lives. They had to use *all* of their senses, from noticing a storm coming to being aware of when they were being watched in the darkness.

This rune is about the power of being human, the human spirit. Think of all those videos of people going above and beyond to rescue a kitten stuck in a hole, or proposals of marriage that make your heart melt, or acts of heroism or faith that make you feel good about being human. These are all part of humanity.

All the horrid stuff is too – let's not put rose-coloured glasses on.

There is a more mystical aspect as well: the *magic* that humans hold, be it *Galdur* or Sithur, or the magic of being able to shape metal or create music. The magic of being human. This magic is what attracts Mannaz.

Odin and Freya are often represented as archetypes of this rune, as they embody that magic – all the beauty, lust, leadership, war, knowledge, spiritual journeying and being in charge. Mannaz brings all those human traits together in both the positive and the negative.

Mannaz here and now
Here and now, the power of humanity has run rampant – power, privilege and entitlement prevail.

The power of Mannaz now is in connecting to ourselves to ensure we have the resources, internally and externally, to make sure our planet continues to function.

Here and now, we get to choose how we show up as humans, and by doing that, we increase our power. The energy we choose can be the personal physical energy that we build in the gym and/or the spiritual energy we gain while in meditation or prayer. Each type of energy builds our human power in different ways. For the last few hundred years, we've been very good at the physical aspects of humanity. Now is our chance to build the energy we need to bring ourselves to a 'higher', more evolved way of operating.

Remember, though, that Mannaz is not just about individuals, but the seven billion people on the planet *as well as* all who have gone before and will come after. Change may seem impossible, but the imbalance of Mannaz in the here and now *can* be corrected through tiny, incremental changes. For example – a very mundane example – lifting weights. We can't all break world records the first time we go to the gym, and getting ripped abs doesn't come overnight. (I kind of wish it did, though.) Instead, muscle power comes through devotion to building and moving the body. Spiritual strength is built the same way, through meditation: the more we do it, the better we become at it.

Basically, Mannaz is our ability to be a conduit of universal energy. So, connecting with the insubstantial energy of the world, feeling what is happening and predicting future events are all Mannaz magic too.

In our personal world, Mannaz is becoming aware of where our problems are and working with our awesome human abilities to be better, to do better.

Building a relationship with Mannaz

Mannaz is a powerful rune to use to build your relationship with your personal power and magic. There are a few traditional ways of doing this, but we are all unique, including in how we connect to the awesome powers that we are born with, and if what I suggest here doesn't work for you, know that there are infinite ways for you to access your power. Just experiment and play. That's how the ancients did it.

❖ The first thing is to get your physical body strong. I don't mean strong like a bodybuilder, but fit and healthy enough to live your life without worrying about whether you can walk upstairs or run for a bus. Our physical form is where we hold our spiritual energy. So the more honed your body becomes to the life you want to live, the more you will find your spiritual energy, your magic, your *Ond*, is able to flow. This isn't to say that you have to be a complete specimen of health and wellness in order to use your magic; it's to encourage you to optimize your body to live the life you want in the way you want and to channel your energy and magic in the way that you require. You know your limits; work with them. But every time you improve yourself, physically, mentally or emotionally, you will find, when you pay attention, that your *Ond* will flow into new areas. You may become better at reading people, for example, or being an oracle, or find you are able to develop mediumship, or become a medical intuitive. By improving your physical vessel in your own unique way, you will improve your spiritual energy too.

❖ Draw, paint or mark the Mannaz rune on your workout log or gym bag. Put it on your meal prep sheet. Use it in places and on things that help you become more yourself – the self that your soul is drawing you towards along the paths of the *Wyrd*.

❖ Adding the Mannaz rune to things that are important to you and that you have with you all the time will aid you in becoming the powerful spiritual human that you are. I have it on the inside of my watch strap and on a pendant. It fits nicely on lifting gloves or a skipping rope. I also put it on the ritual objects I create, like statues to gods or offering bowls.

When Mannaz shows up

In both a reading and in the wild, Mannaz is a call to action for the spiritual, magical self. When you see it, trust your intuition and look for the subtle signs of the energy influencing you. Do three magpies keep showing up? Or several runners with the same hat? What is the universe, or your magical self, trying to tell you?

In a reading, where is the client ignoring the call of the spirit? The call of the *Wyrd*? This rune is pointing to a deficiency in their spiritual or physical energy. There will be clues to where this is in the question.

Mannaz meditation

Let's get down to business. This meditation is a physical one. You are going to need a yoga mat or something similar, a timer and your journal.

❖ Write or draw Mannaz three times in your journal. Then spend a couple of minutes getting yourself into the Mannaz mindset by bringing your focus to what you are going to accomplish.

❖ Now you are going to plank. If you've managed to avoid this in life so far, bad luck, you are going to do it now. Lie on your mat, or the floor, on your tummy, forearms pointing forward, elbows on the floor, toes digging in.

❖ Now lift yourself up off the floor with the strength in your tummy. Hold the position for 10 seconds and chant, 'Mannaz.' You can do it under your breath.

❖ Give it a couple of goes. You can adapt by having your arms straight and fingers pointing forward, or your knees on the floor. If your body simply doesn't do the plank, adapt it as you wish, either with your knees down, or standing with your hands on a wall and your feet slightly further out.

❖ This meditation works by stressing your body ever so slightly, so you can build its power. So, start with 10 seconds, then up the time if you want. I suggest three holds of your plank and then a couple of minutes to journal what you are feeling.

Affirmation

'I am powerful.

LAGUZ

Lah-gooz

Sound
The 'luh' in 'lake' or 'little'.

Inspiration
Face the depths of the unknown.

Gift
Life, health.

Challenge
Stagnation.

Old rune poem

Lagu byþ leodum langsum geþuht,

gif hi sculun neþan on nacan tealtum and hi sæyþa swyþe bregaþ

and se brimhengest bridles ne gym[eð].

Water seems lasting to the liegemen
if they venture out in a tossing barque, so
frightening are the waves of the sea,
and the surf-steed no longer takes care of the
bridle.

There are lots of *Cennings* here, mainly that Laguz is water. Water is one of the prime requirements of life: air, water, food. We can build on them to meet every need we have in life. But without them, we die. In this respect, Laguz is life.

Even now, humans love living by the sea – I know I do – mainly because it's a good source of food and makes travel relatively easy. Especially if you are going to the village across the bay. Or in the Nordic world-view, across the fjord. Fjords are comparatively smooth and much easier to cross than mountains.

The fear of water comes from a time when boats were 30 metres (98 feet) long at most, the waves on the open sea correspondingly huge, and the depths of the oceans unimaginable. The same, depth-wise, could be said of the fjords – the Sognefjord is over 1,000 metres (3,280 feet) deep in places. Not knowing what was below was a hazard in open water, and the sheer size of potentially curious whales and squid was intimidating.

In a way, water itself is intimidating to this day. It can outlast anything that people make. It eats through rock and metal, devours wood and turns the hardest ground to mush. There is power in it, and the ancient Nordic people knew that. The poem speaks of the fear of the sea in the barque steed. This is the fear of surrendering to the sea in a wooden boat. Part of the blessing of Laguz, and the challenge, is facing the fear, and healing through this confrontation. In this way, Laguz is a healer – not in a soft, gentle way, more in a jump from the sauna into the icy water kind of way.

Being stuck in our own fear, sickness or mire won't help us to heal and grow. This rune challenges that stickiness, and promotes healing and wellbeing.

Laguz here and now

Now we know that if we aren't hydrated, we don't think properly, heal properly or function properly. So, Laguz is life. When we are hydrated, we can live life better. Our body works better, our mind works better. Everything is better.

In modern life, Laguz's healing aspect is shown through the healing ability of IV fluids and other liquid medicine. This goes beyond the clinical, though. We now know our body and mind make more of the happy chemicals when we are immersed in water, especially cold water. Free water swimming is an effective treatment for depression and anxiety. This healing Laguz energy accesses the very primal parts of the human physiology and neuropsychology. Don't go cold water swimming without doing the prep work first, though. Find a club.

Building a relationship with Laguz

❖ *Through healing:* Laguz is a powerful healing ally, especially when it comes to the deep healing required for mental health injuries. When I was a nurse, I put it on the back of my ID badge. Laguz is great on any tools you use to heal. It's on my water bottle, so I get a gulp of its resonance every time I drink.

❖ *As a solvent:* The ability of water to wash away all things and dilute them into passivity is a powerful magical energy. There is nothing the sea cannot remove, so when you have an emotional or energetic block, Laguz is a good energy to use to erode or dissolve it.

When Laguz shows up

Laguz showing up in the wild implies there are depths for you to explore, either emotionally or spiritually. Any deep-dive exploration of the self will involve a release of fear so that healing can occur. So Laguz in the wild could be a warning, readying you for what's to come. Alternatively, it could simply be a warning that you're about to get wet. Or that rain is forecast, so take an umbrella with you!

In a reading, Laguz implies healing is needed. Depending on your client's question, look a bit deeper. Is there a wound there, or an ignored fear? Look to where fear is playing on the client's mind and conscience and see how it can be faced and healed.

Laguz meditation

Here are two meditations for you. They are physical meditations. Please adapt them to suit your needs.

❖ The first is to drink water, I use a steel bottle with Laguz stamped onto it; if you wish, you could draw the rune on a bottle or use a sticker. Aim to get three to four litres (around seven pints) a day. It takes this much to ensure you pee clear, which means your body is well hydrated and can remove all toxins effectively. Soda, juice or alcohol doesn't count – it must be water.

❖ The second meditation is to immerse yourself in water – a bath, a lake, a river, the sea. Floating free is powerful magic and I encourage you to experience it. If you are going outside, though, please make sure you are safe. Look for local guidance on free water swimming.

Affirmation

'I can flow like healing water.'

INGWAZ

Ing-Waz

Sound
'ing' as in 'ring' or 'sing'.

Inspiration
Creation demands sacrifice.

Gift
New growth.

Challenge
Self-obsession.

Old rune poem

Ing wæs ærest mid East-Denum gesewen secgun,

oþ he siððan est ofer wæg gewat; wæn æfter ran;

ðus Heardingas ðone hæle nemdun.

> *Ing was first among the east Danes,*
>
> *so he was looked at, until he went to the east on the wave after his wagon,*
>
> *thus these proud men named this hero.*

One of the fun parts of Nordic myth, if you like headaches, is that the stories come from subtly different cultures – the Saxon, Jute, Angle, Dane, Swabian, Langobard, Norse, Icelandic, Frisian, and so the list goes on (and not in chronological order, you purist). In some of the stories there is a god called Ing, though in other, very similar stories, he has the name Frey.

Ing-Frey is very interested in fertility, in ways that only a pre-Christian fertility god can be: he is all about the phallus. Ingwaz carries the energy of fertility, of new growth, of the cycle of life. It is the rune of the creative process, self-development and growth. We have words for these concepts now, but back in the day they were more what you did: you worked to be strong, you made art to make art, you planted seeds, carried water, chopped wood. You did what was necessary for life.

Ing was a hero, and in the early medieval period heroes showed us how to be, how to act and what to strive for. The culture wasn't one of consumerism, or the quick fix, but one of steady progress leading to change. When it took weeks to make a plough and days to plough a field, rushing things was likely to cause problems you didn't want. So, Ingwaz is the rune of making yourself heroic in small increments, one step at a time.

Ingwaz here and now

Today, fertility and creativity are of great importance. We've been trained to be stressed and anxious. When we let the energy of Ingwaz be present, we can use the energy that we were giving to our less useful emotional states – stress, anxiety, burnout – to create and innovate. This is the magic of Ingwaz. By transmuting compost and dark matter into creativity, it can help us become the hero/ine we want to be. Ingwaz is the rune of self-development, of self-improvement, of the creative act and the creative process. Because Ing-Frey wasn't just interested in the act of fertilization, he was interested in the whole process: the process of creative expression.

Ingwaz aids all aspects of growth, from growing window-box chillies to tending raised beds, creating life in the womb, creating art, writing a book, having awesome sex, learning a dance routine that expresses your passion. It's the 'Let's make life fun!' rune.

Building a relationship with Ingwaz

Using this rune to help creation, in whatever form, is awesome.

❖ *Self-improvement:* Ingwaz on your journal or pen will help your creative flow. I have it on my notebook cover. It also finds its way into any learning notes I make or tools I use to learn.

❖ *Art:* Draw Ingwaz on your pencil case, on the back of canvases or behind the drawing in traditional art. Its distinctive shape means it is easily integrated into modern art, as straight lines are everywhere in our world.

❖ *Fertility:* Ingwaz is a rune that will increase fertility, both yours and your partner's, and using body paint will help that aspect of life. You can work it out from there. I use Ingwaz on rune sticks for people who are going through the IVF process or struggling with amenorrhea or erectile dysfunction. Ingwaz loves to support growth and actively encourages fertility and fecundity.

❖ *Creative projects:* Ingwaz is the seed, and using its energy to begin creative projects ensures an efficient start. The potential carried in the seed is the energy of life, and creation is life.

When Ingwaz shows up

Ingwaz in the wild is an invitation to start a creative process, to begin a project, sow a seed. Or, if you've already started, to bring more attention and focus to the project.

To be clear, any and all creativity is being called on here. So, plant the avocado seed, plant the chillies, load up the drawing app, paint the wall. Create. Create a new, improved you. Take a course, dance like no one is watching, hug a tree. Do it all.

In a reading, Ingwaz implies an element of creativity is called for, either by thinking outside the box, bringing more creativity to the question or developing it in some way to reach a goal. Ingwaz is a calling to do better, be better, create more.

Ingwaz meditation

This is a movement meditation, so you will need a yoga mat, a timer and your journal. Hold each position for three minutes. Or, as with all movement, whatever you are comfortable with.

✦ Write your intention for creativity or fertility in your journal and write or draw Ingwaz three times.

✦ There is a breath pattern for this meditation. It's called the 'O' breath. Simply breathe in and out of your mouth, with your mouth in an 'O' shape, like the rune.

✦ Start on your knees and drop back so your butt is on your heels and your hands are stretched out in front of you. In Child's Pose for you yoga enthusiasts. Spend one minute here, doing your 'O' breaths.

✦ Come to a sitting position, stretch your legs out in front of you, just wider than your hips, put your hands on the floor behind you, and lean back on your arms. You are opening your chest to the sky.

❖ Now do your 'O' breaths for another minute.

❖ Next, sit up cross-legged and place your hand in an 'O' shape over your genitals or womb space. Do 'O' breaths for another minute.

❖ Hands to heart, right over left and flat to your sternum, do 'O' breaths for another minute.

❖ Right hand palm up under your heart, left palm down just above your heart, do 'O' breaths for another minute.

❖ Left hand palm to heart, right hand as far around your back as you can get it towards your heart space, do 'O' breaths for another minute.

❖ Then relax. Relax your breath, relax your body.

❖ Then journal anything that came up.

Affirmation

'I create myself into being.'

ᛟTHALA

Oth-al-la

Sound
The long 'oh' or 'oo' sound in 'Odin', 'owl' and 'coup'.

Inspiration
I am the product of the love of millions.

Gift
Family/friends.

Challenge
Insular thinking.

Old rune poem
Eþel byþ oferleof æghwylcum men,
gif he mot ðær rihtes and gerysena
on brucan on bolde bleadum oftast.

A home is loved by each man,
If there the moot holds, and he enjoys justly
and often the convenience of his sweet home.

The cultural appropriation of Nordic culture

This rune is potentially problematic. Modern fascist groups are attempting to culturally appropriate it for their own twisted and evil agenda. But it is not and never has been about genetics or 'pure bloodlines'. I vehemently resist this hate-filled cultural appropriation of Nordic culture.

Þessi hamar brestur fasista. This hammer smashes fascists.

In the Dark Ages, the family was a powerful resource. Indeed, the Icelandic sagas were the wild west of European history, with blood feuds and family wars and all kinds of events based on who was married to whom, but with giant axes rather than six-shooters, and little ponies rather than horses.

In this context, our family are not only those who share our home, but those who live near us, share the same trials and tribulations, share resources and build a community. The rune poem speaks of meetings, *moots* in Old English, and enjoying the hearth. Hearth and home were important to the early medieval people, as the home was a safe space in a hostile world – maybe not safe from people, but from the weather and predators that would kill and take the farm animals that the community depended on – and the hearth was where people slept and shared food and drink, often with animals.

Lots of people living in a relatively small place meant harmony had to be maintained as much as possible. Othala is the harmony of the home.

In the Nordic world, the lady of the house had all the power – she had the wealth, the animals and the ability to divorce her husband if he annoyed her. Othala looks somewhat like a *very* stylized woman, if you make your mind super crude and focus on her tummy and legs. This is the matriarch rune, holding the clan, the family, the community together. The matriarch's word is law. But she may allow you to sleep in the warm with a full belly.

The ancient power of Othala, the hearth where you can be warm and safe and know that your needs are met, is a mixture of Fehu and Nauthiz, Ingwaz and Gebo. In the Dark Ages, fear of the unknown was huge. Home meant love and safety.

Hospitality was super important too and poems were written about how hosts and guests should behave. Visitors were valued, as travelling 20–30 miles in a day was a massive achievement on foot, and almost as impressive on a tiny pony, and they often brought information, trade goods and new interactions. They would be granted a bed and food and, depending on how rich the home was, and the status of the guest, clothes and other gifts would often be given too. In return, the guest would be expected to tell the hall all the news from further afield.

Welcoming others into your home, feeding them and looking after them are all expressions of Othala. As is shutting your doors out of fear of attack. This was a very real possibility in the ancient north, especially when resources were scarce. So, Othala is also about being able to defend your home from aggressors and depend on your community to help you hold what others might take.

Othala here and now

Nowadays we're a global community. Indeed, my closest friends are over 50 miles away – a long way by English standards. Others are in different time zones, and my family are scattered across the world. This doesn't make for a cohesive community able to defend me should a bear or raiding party arrive. So today Othala is the community and family we choose to build around us and call in. It's the energy we exert to look after them and they exert to look after us. It's still our hearth, but it is vastly different from the hearth of 1,500 years ago. Today we build our communities digitally, even our work communities, with working from home being more common. But that means our energetic and physical bodies don't get the same input from our families and communities.

In the Nordic tradition, there is a concept of ancestors of blood, bone and spirit. Ancestors of blood are those who are related to us; ancestors of bone are those to whom we can relate; and ancestors of spirit are the deities, spirits and mythological figures to whom we are drawn. This distinction means that as an empowered human being, we can choose where we draw energy and support from. We are stuck with our family, but we can draw inspiration from historical figures who have the traits we would like to bring to ourselves and our hearth.

Building a relationship with Othala

Building a relationship with Othala is a powerful process, and one that can be as troubling as it is enlightening.

+ *Find your blood ancestors:* First you can delve into your family tree to find your ancestors of blood. There are all kinds of ways to do that

+ *Find your bone ancestors:* This is just as or even more powerful. Putting the photo of someone you admire on your altar, or somewhere you see it a lot, is a great way of bringing that energy into your life.

+ *Build your personal hearth:* Do this in a way that resonates with you, whether that involves digital communication or actually hugging someone and sitting on the sofa drinking cocoa/wine/mead/ whatever feels good to you.

❖ *Have a welcoming home:* Welcoming visitors is a powerful way of building a relationship with Othala. You don't have to clothe everyone who comes to your door, but offering shelter and sustenance to your friends and family builds Othala energy. Reaching out with a letter, phone call or email also builds this kith and kin relationship in our dispersed society.

❖ *Give to charity:* Othala is also the energy of giving to charities that resonate with our values, especially charities that provide shelter and nourishment.

❖ *Place the rune in your home:* Put it above your hearth if you have a fire in your home, or your oven if you don't. Othala is also a potent rune to place where people gather together in your home, maybe by the TV, as living rooms tend to focus on that area, or on the dining table, as people share food there.

When Othala shows up

❖ Where are family ties being activated?

❖ How is home life influencing life in general?

❖ What ancestral energy could be supportive?

❖ Where could family or friends be of benefit?

Othala in the wild is a call to look to your hearth, to the energy of your home. Is it harmonious or does it require work? Where could you be more welcoming? Where are you being *too* welcoming?

Perhaps Othala is reminding you to look to your ancestors of blood, bone and spirit. You may not be in harmony with where you want to be. Or maybe it's directing you to lessons that your ancestors have learned, so that you don't have to learn them the hard way this lifetime.

In a reading, Othala implies that the client's home and hearth require attention. Or that there is someone in their kith and kin who needs attention in some way.

Othala meditation

This meditation can be done with small children, as it's part of the general family vibe. It works with every other family variation too. Family is family.

You'll need your journal, a timer and something to sit on.

- ❖ Sit comfortably. I use a bolster. Children sitting on laps works well here too. Set your timer for three minutes.

- ❖ Put your dominant hand on your heart and say, 'My heart, I love you.'

- ❖ Place your dominant hand on your eyes and say, 'My eyes, I love you.'

❖ Move to the top of your head and say, 'My head, I love you.'

❖ At the navel point say, 'I love you.'

❖ And finally placing both hands on your knees, say, 'I love you.'

❖ Repeat the process for three minutes on whomever you are bringing the blessing to, depending on the age of your children, if you are bringing it to them, and their interest level.

❖ To finish, inhale and exhale slowly through your mouth, wrap your arms around your body and give yourself a big hug. Then hug your family/friends.

❖ Journal what came up.

Affirmation

'I choose my family.'

DAGAZ

Dah-Ghaz

Sound

The 'd' in 'dog', 'dagger' or 'doughnut'.

Inspiration

The potential in the new.

Gift

A new chance.

Challenge

Never staying in the present.

Old rune poem

> *Dæg byþ drihtnes sond, deore mannum,*
>
> *mære metodes leoht,*
>
> *myrgþ and tohiht eadgum and earmum, eallum brice*

> *Day is sent by the Lord, mankind beloved,*
> *glorious light of the Creator,*
> *joy and hope for the rich and the poor, useful*
> *to all.*

I'd like you to think about light. How are you reading/ listening to this now? By artificial light? Is electricity powering your device? Back in the day there was no artificial light beyond oil lamps and candles. Work quite literally stopped when the sun went down. So the new day dawning quite literally meant the possibility of new beginnings.

It also brought relief from the fear of the creatures that dwelt in the darkness and the ability to see what you were actually doing. This daytime energy of Dagaz is the power that comes from being able to interact with your environment in the best way possible. Remember, the further north you go, the shorter the nights get during the summer, and the longer they get during the winter. For the ancient people of the north, daylight was to be treasured.

They also saw transitions as times/places of magic. Dawn/dusk, the seashore, doorways, tunnels – places and times that were not quite one thing and not quite another held power. Anything that had an element of being in two worlds held power. Dagaz is the transition from one state to another – from night to day, from day to night. This energetic shift is the power behind this rune, and what it's attracted to.

Moving from one state to another is also an initiation. Dagaz is the rune of initiation.

Dagaz here and now

Now, Dagaz as a light to work and live by has lost its meaning, as electric light is available at the flick of a switch. What Dagaz is today is the transition, the portal between two states. Light and darkness, on and off, that transference point in the middle.

We change states a lot in our modern lives. Work, play, sofa, chill… The list goes on. Whenever we change states, emotionally and physically, we are in the energy of Dagaz.

We change all the time. Think about it. When you go out on a date, you don't wear PJs and a face mask, do you? You dress up – your state changes. And afterwards? You probably don't go to bed in brogues and a three-piece suit, right?

Anytime you change from one thing to another, that's Dagaz. The rune is attracted to that harmonic resonance of change. Of illumination.

When we learn something, when we make a change, we have to work to embody that change. We have to pass through our own doorways and meet the criteria to do so before our energy bodies and mental bodies will let our psyche realize we've changed. No use telling everyone you're a power-lifter if you've never been to the gym.

When we change completely, we pass through a doorway that signals that change to our whole being.

Dagaz is the doorway, the barrier, that must be crossed to achieve greatness.

Building a relationship with Dagaz

Much is said about working in the light or doing the work of the light. This is good, but what if you stood in the transition between light and darkness? This is the power of Dagaz: the ability to sit in the darkness and transition into the light. You can access this transformational power and use it to grow and develop the best possible version of yourself.

❖ *Overcome limitations:* When you encounter a limitation in yourself that you would like to change, see it as a doorway, an initiation. Use the transitional power of Dagaz to change your state from someone who is under-resourced, despondent and unable to achieve a goal to someone who is resourced, confident and effective.

❖ *Initiate change:* Dagaz on your altar or in your wallet or purse will help you to build this transitional energy and initiate your next change or take you into the next day.

❖ *Ease transitions:* Transitions aren't always pleasant. When I was talking to my wife about this energy, she likened it to the time just before her menstrual bleed, when her temper is short and her tolerance is low, and then she transitions into the next phase of her cycle and is bleeding and in flow, and there's an ease that is available to her. Dagaz is there to ease transitions. The energy may not help with tension or cramps, but it will help with the energetic shift.

When Dagaz shows up

In the wild, Dagaz is a call to change from one state to another or to get ready to change. Look to where you're consciously ready to move, but unconsciously you've not moved yet. Dagaz wants to make the transition as easy as possible, and the rune turning up implies that there is a portal, a door, a transition point coming up for you.

In a reading, Dagaz implies that the client has a line to cross or a point of change to meet. Look at this energy in the context of the question. Are they looking for love? Do they need to change a part of themselves before that can happen? The same for work and other areas.

Dagaz meditation

For this rune meditation you will need a candle, something to light the candle with, your journal, a timer and an eye mask or something to cover your eyes. I use a pair of clean socks.

This is all about transition, the movement between two states.

✦ Draw or write the Dagaz rune in your journal three times.

✦ Lie down, get comfy and set your timer for three minutes. Make sure the candle and lighter are close by.

✦ Cover your eyes and lie in the darkness for three minutes.

✦ When the alarm sounds, light the candle and write down the experience you have had in the transition from darkness to light.

Affirmation

'I am allowed to change.'

THE BLANK RUNE

The blank rune came into rune lore in the 1980s. It first appeared in Ralph Blum's *The Book of Runes* and he based the idea on a set of runes he bought in the 1970s, which had an extra rune. He decided not to see this as a spare, or a print overrun, but as a mystical New Age rune, a '*Wyrd* rune'.

So, essentially the whole concept is based on a tourist souvenir from the 1970s. While some modern ideas, like the *Aettir*, are good and useful, this one adds needless confusion and speculation. I don't see it as valid in reading the runes. I believe that all the runes are *Wyrd* runes.

Part III

HOW TO WORK
WITH THE RUNES

Chapter 4

Reading the Runes

The runes are a very effective oracle, and when they're used as such, they utilize the Norns' and the *Wyrd*'s most potent tool: fate.

Runic energy is that of attraction – the runes are attracted to the energy they are associated with. This means that when they are used for divination, the runes themselves aren't coming up, it's the energy that they are attracted to that is present, and the runes are illuminating that energy. It's kind of like fishing: the right bait catches the right fish. The right energy catches the right rune.

As with the *Völva*, your role when reading the runes is to tap into the energy of the *Wyrd* and interpret them in a way that makes sense to you and your client/friend/ partner/cat. Draw on the threads of the *Wyrd* to build your own resonance with the runes that you are reading.

Runes have been around for a long time, over 1,700 years, in a form that has remained relatively static for over 1,000 years, mainly due to the introduction of Christianity, and this lack of evolution means the energy that they are attracted to can be quite alien to the modern mind. The hard part of reading the runes is working out how our modern ideas fit with the old and entrenched concepts. But the associations of the runes will help us turn those ancient thought patterns into ones that work more coherently in the world we live in now.

By now I'm hoping you've had the chance to experience the energy of each rune. There are lots of concepts and possibilities within each one, so don't feel that you have to know them all off by heart. The runes are practical, mystical and ever-unfolding. What I am sharing is to support you in building your own relationship with them.

My invitation now is for you to put what you've learned so far into practice, so let me share some of the many ways in which you can work with the runes, from daily throws to readings, spells and stavs. Stavs are carved runes on wood or bone, and are used to hold magical energies that can heal or influence other people's actions.

How to build focus

Focus is a powerful tool with any spiritual practice. It involves changing your state to one that's receptive to the energies of the universe.

Set your intention

When reading the runes, your intention is the question you are going to ask. The best way to make sure the energetic pathways are there is to write it out three times in your journal. This allows the energy to flow freely.

Guidance questions are good; yes/no questions not so useful. 'What can I do about Jim at work?' is a good one, as is: 'How can I make this project work better?' I'd steer away from: 'Does Jim at work love me?' That answer will get clouded with emotions and you definitely won't get a yes/no, more an essay on the inner workings of Jim's heart, which will be useless without the context.

Get ready to read and receive

It's not useful to try and read runes when you are excited or distracted, as the fuzzy energy can get in the way. So, prepare yourself first:

❖ Make sure you are comfortable and pay attention to your breath. Breathe in through your nose and out through your mouth.

❖ As you do this, reread your intention, the question in your journal, all the time slowing your breath down. Try to aim for a seven-second inhale and an 11-second exhale. I said 'aim', not 'force'.

❖ When you feel your body has relaxed, bring your attention to your fingers and toes and make sure you can feel them. Feel what they are touching.

❖ Look around the room and find five things you can see, four you can hear, three you can touch, two you can smell and one you can taste.

❖ Now you will be in your body and ready to connect with the energy of the runes. Focus on the question and be aware of the sensations your body is picking up. You know yourself, and the more you are able to feel the subtle ways energy plays with your body, the more powerful you will be in your rune reading.

If you are reading for a client, you can ask them to follow your breath and let their energy field align with yours. It will make your reading that much more powerful.

Casting the runes

I'm going to cover two ways of casting the runes here: the rune cast and the runic draw.

The rune cast

❖ Before you cast, write down your question three times in your journal, so you have a clear idea of what you are asking.

❖ Then sit on the floor, maybe on a cushion or sheepskin, and stretch your legs out in front of you, feet as wide as is comfortable.

❖ Get focused.

❖ Give your runes a good shake and throw them gently at a point just before your knees.

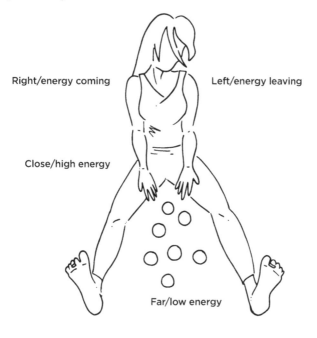

Right/energy coming

Left/energy leaving

Close/high energy

Far/low energy

Interpretation

Runes tend to be on discs or stones that have a blank side and a rune side. Blank side up is a 'not present' reading; rune up, that energy is there. Runes can fall upside down or back to front, but that doesn't matter. If they are visible, their energy is there.

The closer to your power point (your pelvis) a rune is, the more present and potent its energy is, and the further away, the less potent – either coming or just gone.

I feel that the left side is the past, or energy leaving, and the right side is the future, or energy coming. This may be different for you. Test it and see.

Now see which energies are attracted to your question. Remember you are their conduit, so your unconscious bias will be present in them. Setting this aside and becoming a 'hollow bone' to receive guidance is a powerful skill.

The second way I like to draw runes is to ask a direct question and draw a rune to answer it. This is much less 'space intensive' than the first method and you don't end up with runes everywhere. There is nothing more annoying than losing a rune under the sofa and not realizing.

I use this method when I'm doing readings with my clients, for both coaching and divination. It was also used a lot when writing this book.

The runic draw

+ Start with your bag of runes and your question written out three times in front of you.

+ Reach into the bag and draw a rune. This rune is the main answer to the question.

Interpretation
The answer tends to be limited in context initially, so you can draw a second or third rune to expand on the first.

Remember, though, to interpret the reading through the lens of the first rune.

Example of a rune reading

Question: Should I pitch this book to Hay House?

This is in my journal three times in front of me.

First rune: Uruz: Strength, power, stubbornness.

This is less than useful to me right now. What does it mean? I'm big and strong and stubborn already...

Draw a second rune.

Second rune: Ansuz: Speech, inspiration, knowledge.

This, through the lens of Uruz, implies my strength here will be to use my knowledge and words.

This is looking promising. I can pitch this book, using my ability to communicate.

Third rune: Nauthiz: Need, survival, action.

Well, if this isn't a literal call to action for survival, I don't know what is. To survive I'll need to use my language and strengths to get this book to the right person so that they commission it.

And that was how I used my runes to pitch this book...

Context is everything when it comes to runic energy, so make sure you are specific with the questions that you ask. Nebulous questions will get fuzzy answers. Be clear and direct. The runes like that – strong and direct is the Viking way. They aren't very good with subtle hints or suggestions. You can't be subtle when carving your intention into a rock, as was the case with the first runes.

Using Tarot spreads with the runes

One of the good things about the runes is that you can work with them to fit the constructs of modern society too. They have strong roots that are firmly established in history and mythology. With such powerful roots, new branches, new practices, can grow. One of these is reading the runes with a Tarot spread.

A quick internet search will give you lots of Tarot templates to use, but here are some examples to get you started:

Situation, Challenge, Solution

A three-rune draw that works well is 'Situation, Challenge, Solution'.

+ Write your question out three times in your journal.

+ Then focus.

+ Then draw the first rune. This is the crux of the current situation.

✤ The second rune is the challenge. Place the second rune to the right of the first.

✤ And the third rune is the solution. Place the third rune to the right of the second.

An example

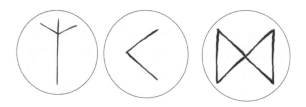

The question is: 'What do I need to do to get the work promotion?'

First rune: Algiz: Defence, barriers

Second rune: Kenaz: Illumination, light in the darkness

Third rune: Dagaz: Change, initiation

Remembering the question at all times, my interpretation of the reading is this:

The first rune implies there is a barrier up, perhaps between how people interact with the client or vice versa, or perhaps a barrier that is more technological. Perhaps a missed email?

The second rune is the challenge, and not seeing everything that is around you is the challenge of Kenaz, so has the client been blind to what is happening around them? Is someone working in the shadows to further their own agenda? Is there something structural going on with the company that the client has not seen? 'There is a barrier caused by not seeing what is going on,' would be my interpretation of these first two runes.

The third rune is the solution, and Dagaz is change and initiation, so what does the client need to change to get promoted? This depends on their insights from the first and second runes. They could choose to go looking for technological and hidden things that are stopping them from getting promoted. Is the company behind in tech and therefore not competitive in the market? Is there a skill they themselves are lacking that is a barrier to their advancement?

Remember that the runes are open rather than subtle. They can point to subtle things, but they don't hide information. Any subtlety is in your interaction with them and with the client.

Chapter 5

Runic Spells

Runes are letters, and what do we do with letters? We spell words. This is how we harness energy with runic sticks and binds, stavs or Sithur. Runic spells are ways of bringing specific energies to bear on a situation.

Here is an example from 'Egil's Saga', the story of an adventuring Viking shared during the height of the Viking Age. Egil was a hero in the Viking mould: mysterious, powerful and a user of magic.

Egil ate his fill and then went to where the woman lay stricken. He talked with her. He then commanded that the bed linen and clothes be changed for fresh under her.

When under the bed he found a shard of bone, with the rune carved on it.

He read the runes and remembered them and cast

the bone into the fire. He then burned all the old
bed clothes and the ladies' old dirty clothes.

He then sang:

A man should not rush to carve the runes
Unless he can do it with cunning
It will be too much power for a man
Especially if the rune is wild and dark
The many layers of power of the runes ten
The strong flowing woman
Can hold the grief and pain

Egil's Saga, chapter 73
translation by Richard Lister

So, Egil, a rune master, discovered the runes that were in the bed of a sick woman, destroyed them and dissipated the resonant energy.

The runes have power to encourage sickness *and* health, love *and* lust, war *and* peace. *We* get to choose how we work with them and direct their energy.

Runic sticks

Runic sticks are spells that are traditionally written on the wood of a fruit tree, as this is present in the world in two ways. It is not only the giver of life, in the form of fruit, but it can also be cut down and used to make something.

Now I put my health and safety hat on. When you make a runic spell, and I feel you will, make sure you are acting within the scope of your personal skills and abilities.

Don't use sharp implements if you aren't confident using them. Don't use hot things if you aren't competent handling them. You know, take adult responsibility for yourself.

How to make a runic spell

You will need: a lollipop or popsicle stick, a piece of scrap paper and a sharpie, pen or other way of marking the stick.

❖ First come up with the energy you want your spell to bring in. For example, I'm going to suggest confidence.

❖ Then choose the words you want your spell to bring in. Confidence, for example – what makes confidence? Courage? Strength? Stubbornness? Happiness? Spirit? I chose strength, resilience and the ability to adapt.

❖ Now scoot back over to Part II, where the rune descriptions are, and match your words with the runic energy you want. For strength, I chose Uruz; for resilience, I chose Eihwaz; for adaptability, I chose Dagaz.

❖ On your paper, draw the runes five or six times in the order that is pleasing to your eye.

❖ When you are ready, put some atmospheric music on (*see the Resources section for examples if you need them*).

❖ Put your hands on your heart and your tummy.

❖ Take a deep breath and let it out.

❖ In those couple of seconds between the inhale and exhale, feel your connection to you, your body, the ground and the sky all flow over you like a thick coat, supporting you, protecting you and helping you. If you have spirit guides or angels you call on, now is a good time to do so.

❖ Once you feel the energies are right, mark your stick with your three runes. I have several different methods of doing this, depending on how I want the energy to flow:

>> Quick and dirty but effective, like a band aid on a knee, the first method I use is marking the wood with a sharpie, marker pen or even a biro.

>> In a more 'intentful' process, I use a metal stamp set that punches the runes into the wood.

>> Sometimes I use a pyrography tool to burn the runes in. This, for me, is one of the most powerful ways of doing it.

>> Alternatively, you could carve the runes in with a knife or chisel. I keep cutting my fingers when I do this, so I don't do it. Take responsibility for yourself. Don't cut your fingers off, you use them all the time.

❖ When it's done, I thank the gods/goddesses with some cake and/ or mead or wine. If you don't do alcohol, then juice is fine.

Take the paper you planned everything on and burn it. Don't just put it in the bin, as the energy will still be there, and discarding it like a banana skin is disrespectful and could irritate the energy of the cosmos.

Using your stick

Once your stick has been marked, it is an object of power and should be treated as such.

To use it, you can either stick it in your pocket, wallet or purse and carry it with you, or place it under your bed, where you lie down. That way, the energies will be affecting you when you are asleep.

Sticks are like medication: they do the job they were designed to do. That's why they are so powerful. Also like medication, though, there is the possibility of side-effects.

Intent matters here. Creating a stick with the three runes in the example (Uruz, Eihwaz and Dagaz) gives what I feel confidence is. The problems come if I'm not clear with my intent. If I just mark the stick with no intent, the runes themselves will decide what energy to bring. It could be stubbornness, poison and change, and I don't want to put that energy into my system. So be super clear with your intent.

Disposing of your stick

When you've finished using your stick, beware – it's like nuclear waste in that it keeps radiating the energy infused into it. So, please burn it, as the lingering runic energy can spread and cause unintended energetic contamination.

Bind runes

Sticks use the individual energy of each rune to put a spell in place. What I'd like to suggest now is another way of creating spells: rune binding.

Bind runes are more artistic than sticks, and they need more thought, as the constructs can have unintended results. When you make a bind rune, you set an intention and then you call in all the runes that will support that intention and layer them. The shapes will fit together to create the energetic resonance you require.

How to make a bind rune

You'll need a piece of scrap paper, a pen, a piece of wood about 5 cm by 5 cm (2 inches by 2 inches) or a pebble with a flat side, plus something to mark the wood or pebble. Sharpies rock.

✦ Begin by building your focus. Grab your journal and write out three times what you want your bind rune to do. Be super clear and succinct. I'm going to choose protection for a new baby.

✦ Again, pick the runes you want for this energy. I'm going to choose Algiz for protection, Wunjo for happiness and Ingwaz for growing strong.

✦ Take your first rune and make that the base. I like starting with a rune with a straight line in the centre, as I like symmetry. Your bind rune doesn't have to be symmetrical, though, it just has to look good to your eye.

✦ Layer the next rune over your base rune. I used Algiz as it's easy to add another rune to its straight stalk.

✦ Before you continue with more runes, sketch a few designs on your scrap paper, so you know where you're going and can make it look good. I learned in Accident and Emergency that when doing a dressing, the neater and better-looking it was, the better it worked. The same applies to bind runes, so practise on paper first.

✦ Continue building up your bind rune. You can rub out lines as you go and add them in to make the image you find most appealing. You can repeat your rune structure if you wish.

✦ Write down, or remember, the order of the layers and continue building your bind rune in any artistic way you wish – the more beautiful, the better. Remember it doesn't have to be symmetrical. This idea can be quite jarring to our modern sensibilities. Here is the bind rune I've made: Wunjo, Algiz and Ingwaz.

◆   When you've sketched your bind rune and you are happy with how it's constructed, you can put it on your wood or stone. Again, if you aren't comfortable using tools, find another way. Sharpies are a good stop-gap.

Watch for hidden intent

Hidden intent? You may have built your bind rune with the three runes for your intent, but what could be hidden in that bind? Is Isaz there, for example?

Definitely. What other runes have made it into your bind that you didn't mean to have there?

Be mindful of your intent and look for possible energetic side-effects. But remember that this energetic spill can be harnessed to build a more powerful bind rune, bringing in more energy.

The three runes I've given, for example, could easily make Othala as well. That is a good thing – a strong support network will definitely protect the baby.

But what if I accidentally put Hagalaz in there? There would be some big ole baby tantrums.

This is the art of making a bind rune: seeing what energy is attracted as you build your rune and being careful not to bring in any energy that you don't want.

Using your bind rune

Remember that when you have achieved your purpose, you will want to burn the bind rune, so put it on a piece of card or a lollipop stick, and then you can place it wherever it will be most useful. Is it meant to create lust in the bedroom? Put it on the headboard. To foster creativity at work? Put it on your computer monitor. Success at school? On your pencil case or laptop. The list is endless. You decide how you are going to use the energies.

Unbinding

When you've achieved your goal, please destroy your bind rune with fire, as otherwise the runic energy can linger, spread and cause unintended energetic contamination. If you've used a marker pen and a stone, scrub the stone down with some nail polish remover or dish soap to remove the lines. It doesn't have to be absolutely perfect. The intent to remove the bind rune is the important bit. It's this that breaks the magic.

Singing the runes

If you are feeling musical, then when you do things like cook, clean or sew, you could use *Galdur* and sing the runes into the task you are working on to empower it. Sing runes of calm into the family dinner, runes of travel into the car's fuel tank and runes of protection into the baby's car seat.

Feel into the energy of the runes you sing to make them uniquely yours. Uruz is a deep vibration that comes from your gut, Raido is a whoop, Nauthiz is a whisper. Play with the sounds while remembering to pay attention to the energies around you, as when they are right, they will feel right. You will know when you've got your personal rune vibration going.

Unkind or evil use of runes

There is no law of three in the Nordic tradition – the law that what you give out returns to you threefold – but there is the law of returns. What you give out will return to you, so if you build a bind or stick with negative intent, you had better take steps to mitigate the blowback. Remember that for the ancient people of the north, being petty, vindictive or horrible was frowned on, but the law did actually permit revenge.

Asking for guidance from your energetic and spiritual guides and having them on side is always useful for mitigating negative fallout. But the ideal thing is to make sure you don't do to someone what you wouldn't want to happen to you, because your energy is going to be tied up in your *Wyrd*. You made it, after all.

What's Next?

You've taken your first steps on the runic path. What's next?

You may notice that as you spend more time getting to know the runes and building your personal practice, you experience some energetic shifts. You may be drawn to particular deities, for example, or they may be drawn to you. Maybe, like me, you'll see Huginn and Muninn when Odin comes to check you're on the right path.

This shift in your energetic and mental pathways will be substantial and subtle at the same time. Don't be afraid to adapt, adjust, go back, look again, mull over an idea and see how it fits with your world-view.

You might receive instant results – and if you do, don't forget to give an offering of thanks – but don't expect them. Take time to build your relationship with the runes. Then you can deepen it.

Deepening your experience of the runes

There are some extra little nuggets of information that may resonate with you when you are working with the runes. These are things that maybe don't work for everyone, but if they work for you, they can deepen your experience.

Remember what I said at the beginning? About roots? About the deep roots of the runic tradition and the new branches that the rune tree can put forth? There are branches, twigs and leaves aplenty and some are in the table below. It is far from exhaustive, but covers some basic ideas that I've found really useful when working with the runes. The crystal correspondences are divined from my own felt exploration. Use the information as you will, and don't be afraid to add to it, change it, adapt it in whatever way feels best in your experience of the cosmos. I simply ask that you honour what has gone before and is now allowing your play and exploration to be possible.

Rune name	Crystal(s)	Element(s)	Associations
Fehu	amber, moss agate, gold	Fire and Earth	cattle, gold, fire, money, resources, reputation, trade
Uruz	amber, jet	Earth	ox, strength, raw power
Thurizaz	sapphire	Fire	thorn, spike, lightning, strength, piercing

Rune name	Crystal(s)	Element(s)	Associations
Ansuz	emerald	Air	ash, fly agaric mushroom, inspiration, magic, wisdom, speech, oak
Raido	turquoise, chrysoprase	Air	horse, goat, air, basil oil, oak
Kenaz	heliotrope, optical calcite	Fire	worm, owl, red, orange, pine
Gebo	opal	Water	wild pansy, gold, elm
Wunjo	diamond	Air	indigo, butterfly, ash, chamomile, warmth
Hagalaz	onyx	Water and Air	blue, grey, ash tree, hail, water
Nauthiz	lapis lazuli	Fire	tardigrades, beech, pepper, blood red, the colour black
Isaz	Himalayan quartz	Water	reindeer, polar bear, the colour white, ice, snow, the colour black, alder
Jera	carnelian	Earth	eagle, rosemary, pine, green, blue
Eihwaz	topaz	Fire	fire, energy, yew, orange, the bow, benzoin
Peroth	aquamarine	Water	sex, fate, water, luck, pear, apple, fun, games, singing
Algiz	amethyst	Air	elk, swan, green, adaptation, technology
Sowolio	ruby	Fire	peppermint, the shield, gold, eagle
Tiwaz	red coral	Air	the sword, oak, spear, red, thyme

Rune name	Crystal(s)	Element(s)	Associations
Berkanan	moonstone	Earth	birch, renewal, green, moon, squirrel
Ehwaz	optical calcite	Air	ash, apple, white, drumbeat, horse
Mannaz	garnet	Earth and Air	human, raven, fly agaric mushroom, blue
Laguz	salt crystal, pearl	Water	water, the unknown, emotions, blue, boat, seaweed, fjord, sea, lake
Ingwaz	amber	Earth	seed, boar, fertility, phallus, vulva, apple, comfrey
Othala	bloodstone	Fire and Earth	family, ancestry, hearth, yellow, hawthorn, lavender
Dagaz	emerald	Fire	day, rowan, doorway, hawk, linden tree

Here you are stepping beyond the basics and into being a rune practitioner in your own right. So, expand your experience of the runes as you will.

The best part about building your own practice on good strong runic roots is that your branch of knowledge and practice can grow and become your own unique way of working.

With this in mind, don't be afraid to add your personal associations to this table. What resonates with you and a particular rune? Play, experiment and adapt your practice to become the awesome practitioner you know you are.

As you allow your experience of the runes to become *your* practice, while knowing that you are forever connected to the roots of the runic tree, the energy of the *Wyrd* will flow around you. The more you play with, work with and interact with the runic energy, the easier it will be to find your place on the *Wyrd* and build your energy from a place of power.

Remember this energy is more powerful when shared. So, with the wisdom and knowledge you've discovered in this book, please make bind runes, share rune readings and develop rune spreads that help both you and your community.

Speaking of sharing, if you take photos and put them on the internet, please tag me so I can see how awesome you are: @richlisteruk.

And finally...

You've started along the path of connection, study and development, mystical and *Wyrd* coincidences and unfoldments that will mark you as someone who is awake and aware of the web of energy that surrounds us, nurtures us, teaches us and binds us together.

So let's end as we began, around a fire, with the flickering flames and the smell of pine resin, and I now invite you to feel the earth beneath your feet, the sun on your face and the wind in your hair, to hear the sound of the fire crackling in your ears and to smell the pines and know you have all that you need within you to achieve total victory in this life. Whatever that means to you.

Big love

Rich xxx

Resources

For help in deepening your learning, please check out www.richardlister.com and click on 'Runes Made Easy', where you'll find meditations, artwork and links to music.

Here is where to get the drumbeat audios: www.richardlister.com/resources.

Books and text

If you want to look into the stories of the Nordic peoples,do have an internet search for the books below. You can get most of them in physical form.

The Danish Sagas. I can only find these in Danish and online.

The Elder Edda: A Book of Viking Lore, trans. Andy Orchard, Penguin Classics, 2011

The Prose Edda: Tales from Norse Mythology, trans. Jesse Byock, Penguin Classics, 2005

The Sagas of the Icelanders, trans. Jane Smiley, Penguin Classics, 2005

The Saga of the Volsungs: The Norse Epic of Sigurd the Dragon Slayer, trans. Jesse Byock, Penguin Books, 1999

Voluspa, the Viking Prophecy: More Than 1,000 Years Old, Gudrun Publishing, 2006. This one takes some finding. I got mine in a little shop in Paris.

The Wanderer's Hávamál, trans. Jackson Crawford, Hackett Publishing Co. Inc., 2019

Ralph Blum, *The Book of Runes*, Oracle Books, 1982

David and Julia Line, *Fortune Telling by Runes*, The Aquarian Press, 1983

Nigel Pennick, *Runic Astrology: Starcraft and Timekeeping in the Northern Tradition*, The Aquarian Press, 1990

Stephen Pollington, *Rudiment of Rune Lore*, Anglo-Saxon Books, 2008. This is an accessible scholarly book on the runes, and Pollington's re-enactment group, Wulfeodnas, is a joy in early medieval bling: www. facebook.com/Wulfheodenas.

Rune Hjarnø Rasmussen, *The Nordic Animist Year*, Nordic Animism, 2020. Full of great rituals and magic for the whole year.

Terje Spurkland, *Norwegian Runes and Runic Inscriptions*, Boydell and Brewer Ltd, 2009. A detailed book full of runic awesomeness.

Music

Wardruna is a band that has massively influenced how people interact with the runes. Their music can be found anywhere you get music, or at www.wardruna.com. I wholeheartedly recommend them, their music and their message.

Other good examples of *Galdur* are:

❖   Seidr Blot (www.facebook.com/seidrblot)

❖   Heilung (www.facebook.com/amplifiedhistory)

❖   Skáld (www.facebook.com/skaldvikings)

The Scandinavian world

Nordic animism is an underlying tenet of this book and you can find out more from www.nordicanimism.com.

Bergen, Stavanger, Oslo, Birka and Uppsala museums have lots of exhibits on their virtual tours, as do most museums in the Scandinavian world. I especially like the rune stones in Stavanger. Tromsø Polar Museum has some great rock art that is the precursor to runes.

Finally, a warning

Sadly, I have to advise you to be aware, when you are exploring the ancient Nordic tradition, that there is a significant number of fascist agendas tangled with the portrait of that culture. Some people with foolish and fascist ideals are trying to culturally appropriate ancient Nordic symbols and practices, and this needs to be resisted in order to stop the corruption of this amazing history. I condemn those who would take from this powerful and sacred culture in order to spread hatred and violence.

To keep yourself safe while looking at websites about the runes, some key words to be aware of are 'ethno state' and 'white European'. Anything with far-right undertones can be condemned to Niflheim. Reputable sites will let you know who is behind them and clearly condemn the other sort.

A Note from the Author

In 2000 I discovered my spiritual path while working in a conventional healthcare job. I found a group of like-minded people and followed their path. In late 2005 I asked my gods for help in becoming who I was meant to be.

This led to some interesting experiences, including a career as a trained nurse, yoga teacher, massage therapist and shaman, and then training as a coach and working with people with stress disorders.

Most importantly, it led to meeting the love of my life.

And then lockdown happened.

Everything stopped, everything changed. I got Covid-19, then long Covid. As the virus worked its way through my system and the damage it did healed, my physical and psychological weaknesses were exposed. Weaknesses that I'd previously ignored became a raw, aching wound. I had to change.

I changed my diet and how I moved my body. The symptoms increased. So I changed my focus, from the psychological/medical model to the more spiritual. That was where I found my centre, the point from which I could re-emerge.

Still my body and mind were racked with visions and sounds. I couldn't sleep, and I'm a *good* sleeper. Then it dawned on me that the gods I'd asked for help were ready, my mind was ready and my body was... getting there. I had to make more changes. I had to offer something more to the world.

So here I am. Twenty years of evolution, from high-tech emergency medicine to spiritual medicine, poised and ready to help you.

I work with people remotely and in person on what they want to heal and change. And in every aspect of this, I work with the runes.

You can find me at www.richardlister.com or @richlisteruk on social media.

Acknowledgements

I would like to thank and acknowledge the people who have guided me to where I am.

Lisa – my awesome wife, Steve Harrison, The Ragged Dragon and the Universe. Without these combined energies this work would not work.

ABOUT THE AUTHOR

Lisa Lister

Richard Lister is a trained nurse, intuitive body worker, life coach and spiritual guide. He works with clients globally, offering one-to-one sessions, workshops and online coaching, and specializes in embodiment, spiritual resilience and personal connection.

Rich is made from the stuff of Vikings. His interest in all things Norse began at the age of four and he has been reading and working with the runes for 20 years.

 richlisteruk

 @richlisteruk

www.richardlister.com

Listen. Learn. Transform.

Listen to the audio version
of this book for FREE!

Connect with your soul, step into your purpose, and find joy with world-renowned authors and teachers—all in the palm of your hand. With the *Hay House Unlimited* Audio app, you can learn and grow in a way that fits your lifestyle . . . and your daily schedule.

With your membership, you can:

- Expand your consciousness, reclaim your purpose, deepen your connection with the Divine, and learn to love and trust yourself fully.

- Explore thousands of audiobooks, meditations, immersive learning programs, podcasts, and more.

- Access exclusive audios you won't find anywhere else.

- Experience completely unlimited listening. No credits. No limits. No kidding.

Try for FREE!

Visit **hayhouse.com/audioapp** to start your free trial and get one step closer to living your best life.

Hay House Podcasts
Bring Fresh, Free Inspiration Each Week!

Hay House proudly offers a selection of life-changing audio content via our most popular podcasts!

Hay House Meditations Podcast

Features your favorite Hay House authors guiding you through meditations designed to help you relax and rejuvenate. Take their words into your soul and cruise through the week!

Dr. Wayne W. Dyer Podcast

Discover the timeless wisdom of Dr. Wayne W. Dyer, world-renowned spiritual teacher and affectionately known as "the father of motivation." Each week brings some of the best selections from the 10-year span of Dr. Dyer's talk show on Hay House Radio.

Hay House Podcast

Enjoy a selection of insightful and inspiring lectures from Hay House Live events, listen to some of the best moments from previous Hay House Radio episodes, and tune in for exclusive interviews and behind-the-scenes audio segments featuring leading experts in the fields of alternative health, self-development, intuitive medicine, success, and more! Get motivated to live your best life possible by subscribing to the free Hay House Podcast.

Find Hay House podcasts on iTunes, or visit
www.HayHouse.com/podcasts for more info.

HAY HOUSE
Online Video Courses

Your journey to a better life starts with figuring out which path is best for you. Hay House Online Courses provide guidance in mental and physical health, personal finance, telling your unique story, and so much more!

LEARN HOW TO:

- choose your words and actions wisely so you can tap into life's magic

- clear the energy in yourself and your environments for improved clarity, peace, and joy

- forgive, visualize, and trust in order to create a life of authenticity and abundance

- manifest lifelong health by improving nutrition, reducing stress, improving sleep, and more

- create your own unique angelic communication toolkit to help you to receive clear messages for yourself and others

- use the creative power of the quantum realm to create health and well-being

To find the guide for your journey,
visit www.HayHouseU.com.

HAY HOUSE
online learning

HAY HOUSE

Look within

Join the conversation about latest products, events, exclusive offers and more.

 Hay House

 @HayHouseUK

 @hayhouseuk

We'd love to hear from you!